Writing the Land:
Currents

Writing the Land: Currents
Edited by Lis McLoughlin, PhD

Published by NatureCulture LLC
www.nature-culture.net
www.writingtheland.org

ISBN: 978-1-7375740-5-7
First Edition

Cover Artwork: *Corvid I* by Martin Bridge
www.thebridgebrothers.com

Cover and Interior book design: Lis McLoughlin

Other books in this series:
Writing the Land: Foodways and Social Justice (2022)
Writing the Land: Windblown I (2022)
Writing the Land: Windblown II (2022)
Writing the Land: Maine (2022)
Writing the Land: Northeast (2021)

Related volume:
Honoring Nature (2021)

Series/related books publishers: 2022 & 2023 NatureCulture LLC
2021 Human Error Publishing
For more information: www.nature-culture.net

Writing the Land: Currents

Edited by Lis McLoughlin, PhD

Published by
NatureCulture LLC
Northfield, MA

Covenants, a Foreword

In early November of this year, I received word that North Florida's Lake Jackson, one of 22 landscapes featured in this anthology, was entering a dry down.

I drove north to Faulk Landing and instead of swimming or boating, walked far out over the lake bottom. The ground crisped under my boots, speaking to the regional drought that has stalked the Southeast for many hot months.

I found myself on foot among fields of water lilies—where gallinules so recently stepped, pad to pad, on long toes—blanketing the once-upon-a-time lake bottom. The round cheeks of lily leaves were laid against the mud, still held fast by ropy stems, waiting for the water to once again rise. Waiting for the covenant between aquifer and rainfall and sinkhole to refill the lake, as it will.

Sinkhole lakes such as Jackson cyclically dry down after long periods of low rainfall. This geological process balances the water above—rainfall—with water below—the precious aquifer. I walked along a thin braided stream which has found a groove in the lake bed. I heard a rush, a waterfall. I'd arrived at Porter sink, the keyhole between the sky and the underworld. Water pooled at its entrance, and there, four kinds of egrets and herons and two species of ibis darted trapped fishy prey. A bald eagle dropped from the sky, pushing the waders up into the air and landed on the mud to share a fish.

I continued my walk, raising binoculars to the rolling forested hillsides that contain the lake basin. Flights of killdeer, cormorants, turkey vultures, and red winged blackbirds overhead, some silent, some calling each other close.

I breathe in the scent and the sights of this dry but fully living lake.

Within each of the protected landscapes featured in this anthology, natural cycles like Lake Jackson's dry down are allowed to continue their life-giving ways. As we conserve the landscapes, a relationship regrows between people and place. As we protect, we are protected. As we love, we are loved.

Love for a place begins
with your body[...]
Walk quietly and learn from this second growth forest
what it means to be whole.

—from "Seventy Years After the Clearcut: The Keystone" by Vicki Graham (p. 5)

Connecticut poet laureate Margaret Gibson wrote in her poem "Meditation on a Food Plain Meadow Lit and Shadowed by Sun and Cloud" for Great Meadows Conservation Trust (p. 129):

If, with your whole body in sunlight and shadow you read the land,
you may
> *sense a covenant*

that links sycamore, migrant oriole, corn farmer, native pharmacist,
alluvial silts, arrowroot, and black willow

into one flooding of water wind sunlight earth.

Why would you want to alter that covenant?

The aim of this beautiful collection is to elucidate and honor the covenant between people and the land and the waters and wild creatures embraced by 11 far-flung and diverse land trusts stretching from Oregon to Florida. Each landscape's poet has laid their words against the land, hoping to draw ever wider circles of support for the places they love.

Take these poems as a map into place and body, for only in remembering that connection, will we save ourselves and this ancient Earth.

—*Susan Cerulean*
Tallahassee, Florida
November 2022

Preface:
Currents of Creativity

Without Nature, of which we are a part, humans are incomplete. Writing the Land was created to help people be in right relationship with the rest of Nature, and in our third year, reasons to do this work are even more relevant. The Earth needs us to repair and restore some of the damage we've wrought, while human beings still need meaningful contact with the Earth to be our full selves.

In this volume, a wide range of poets from youth to laureates offer themselves as conduits for Nature's voices. Through them, 22 lands from across the country tell their stories of relationships over time with humans and elements, plants and animals.

As poets embodying, communicating, and hopefully enhancing these connections through art, we work in partnership with land conservation organizations to elucidate the many varied ways to conserve land: ethically, practically, artistically, and with joy.

Join us to explore how currents of creativity can enhance our understanding of place and purpose in land conservation.

—*Lis McLoughlin, PhD*
Northfield, MA
November 2022

Photo: Rabbit with Grass by Marty Espinola

WRITING THE LAND: CURRENTS
TABLE OF CONTENTS

WILD RIVERS LAND TRUST

 Oregon

Keeping our wild & working lands forever abundant

Our Vision: We envision a future where clean water, abundant salmon runs, sustainable working lands, and prospering rural communities forever define Oregon's southern coast.

Our Mission: To keep the irreplaceable lands and waters of the southern Oregon coast forever wild and abundant.

-Keystone Nature Preserve: Poet Vicki Graham

Wild Rivers Land Trust

Wild Rivers Land Trust (WRLT) believes our enduring habitats, economic prosperity, and rural coastal culture are interconnected. Our service area includes 2.3 million acres that stretch 135 miles along the southern Oregon coast. From Tenmile Lakes to the Winchuck River, we conserve and steward places people and wildlife depend on for clean air, fresh water, and healthy surroundings. And by partnering with willing landowners, we help working farms, forests, and ranches preserve their legacy for future generations.

Founded in 2000, WRLT has protected thousands of acres of wild lands and waters and provides safe habitat for all species of plants and animals. Our future, that of the planet and the land trust, will depend on the passion instilled for a healthy, sustainable Earth by caring communities, individuals, corporations and agencies.

We invite everyone to read more at wildriverslandtrust.org and we thank you for your support.

By protecting these wild places, we are ensuring a future that will provide habitat for many imperiled species, such as coho salmon, spotted owls, marbled murrelets and many others. We manage our preserves for ecological function—prioritizing restoration and protection of these critical areas. Protecting these natural spaces also provides substantial benefits to our local communities—clean air and water, open green space, carbon storage, as well places to recreate, hunt, and forage. We are committed to the fact that some places are best left wild, forever.

Our conservation work directly benefits:
- Wild salmon, animals, and birds that rely on natural habitat to live their lives, find their food and rear their young
- Plants and animals that need clean, cold water
- Local residents who live, work, and play on the South Coast
- Farmers and ranchers who want to preserve their legacies forever
- People who fish, hunt, hike, swim, paddle, and connect with nature
- Those who care about preserving our world-class wild salmon runs
- Everyone on the southern Oregon coast who relies on clean air, fresh water and wild lands.

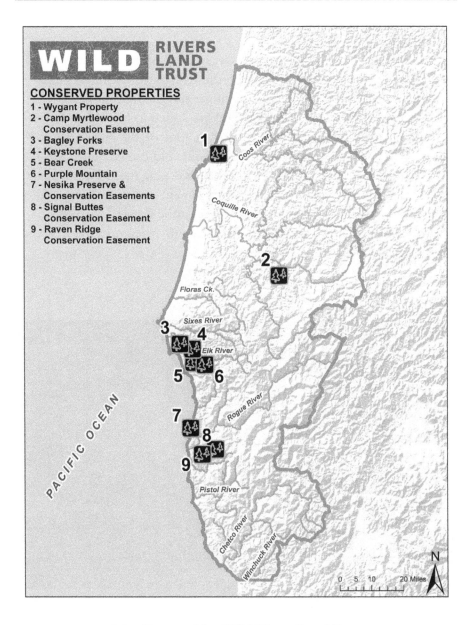

Map Prepared by: Wild Rivers Land Trust
World Terrain Basemap Sources: Esri, USGS, NOAA
Hydrology Map Sources: Oregon Framework Hydrology, USGS

Keystone Nature Preserve

The definition of "keystone" is the fundamental base of a system on which all else depends and in this case the Keystone Nature Preserve completes that perfectly. In 2004, Keystone was the first property acquired by Wild Rivers Land Trust and has added to the lush green corridor along the Wild & Scenic Elk River. One of the great features about Keystone is that the forests will become old-growth and add to the surrounding ancient forests in the area. Keeping these forests intact allows all creatures who rely on this environment a place to live, grow, procreate and sustain undisrupted lives. Keystone Preserve is truly one of those special places that will take your breath away and make everyone realize this is nature at its finest.

Photo: Blue Heron at the Elk River

Seventy Years After the Clearcut: The Keystone
by Vicki Graham

I. A Promise

The story of a forest can begin
anywhere:

with the toothwort's first flower
in February;

with tectonic plates slamming against the Oregon coast
400 million years ago;

with a bear peeling bark from a cedar,
licking the sapwood, tasting the forest's sugar;

with a spring board notch cut in 1950,
still visible today in the stump of a 400-year-old fir;

or with a promise: to create a wildlife corridor
from Cape Blanco to the Siskiyous
and make the forest whole again.

Here, where an old logging road
crumbles and slides off the hillside
into the Elk River,
a sign nailed to a tree tells us
this forest is private land
protected by the Wild Rivers Land Trust:
the Keystone Nature Preserve.

The NE ¼ of the NW ¼;
the SE ¼ of the NW ¼;
the NE ¼ of the SW ¼;
and the NW ¼ of the SW ¼
Lot 3, all in Section 31,
Township 32 South,

Range 14 West of the Willamette Meridian,
Curry County, Oregon.

Legal descriptions, metes and bounds,
property lines drawn on maps,
take us to the land
to trace on foot
not a line of plastic flags
tied around tree trunks
or dangling from huckleberry bushes,
but the contours of a watershed,
a forest clearcut seventy years ago,
now healing itself.

II. Love for a Place

Love for a place begins
with your body: the silk
of willow leaves, the golden flash
of a kinglet's crown,
the pileated woodpecker's drum.

Walk quietly and learn from this second growth forest
what it means to be whole:
the old forest logged and burned
and left to heal itself,
the new forest growing out of the old.

Snags, root balls, rotting stumps, and fallen trees.
Lungwort, sword fern, licorice fern, deer fern,
iris, toothwort, and evergreen violets.
And towering above, Douglas firs
with their deeply fissured bark,
the feathery branches of cedars,
and tanoaks and myrtlewoods heavy with moss.

Vine maples weave counterpoint,
their leaves soft as pleated silk,
opening like hands turned flat
to the sun, catching the light.

Learning a forest
is like learning by ear a piece of music,
each orchid a variation on a theme,
the flower designed for the one insect
that will pollinate it:
the forked lip of heart-leaf twayblade,
the magenta spots of a coralroot,
the rattlesnake plantain's hood.

Study the golden eyes of a tree frog,
trace the elastic strings
of the beard lichens' fibrous lace,
breathe in the sudden scent of chanterelles
after the first rain in September,
taste a huckleberry, and then another
and another, savor the sweet bite
tart on your tongue.

Walk through a myrtlewood grove,
skirt a wetland,
scramble through a tangle of willows on the flood plain
to the gravel bar and the river,
a silk ribbon curling over rock.

whheeet   whheeet   whheeet,
a spotted sandpiper calls,
skittering across the stones—
a broken wing display
luring you away from a clutch of eggs
the colors of river stones
hidden under the willows.

Sit quietly by the river
and feel the heat of the cobble stones.
Look up: fir and cedar,
myrtlewood and tanoak
interweave, green on green on green—
how many words for green do you know?
Does it matter if you can't name them?
Listen for the song of the water ouzel,
the notes clear above the thrum of water on rock,
watch as the ouzel flies upriver.

All of this is safe. Forever.

III. Crossings

We draw boundaries on maps,
run lines, hang flags, post signs
to protect the land.

But the Keystone is not a garden,
and a forest cannot be cordoned off.

Wind and rain sweep through,
and each winter, the river floods, carves a new bed,
and the boundaries meander:
inches or acres of land gained or lost.

Lie flat on the flagged property line
and look into the canopy:
the trees seem to want to touch each other—
branches knitting together,
tracing lace circles against the sky
where there are no lines.

In summer, the ghost pipe rises from the duff,
a silvery cloud of bell-shaped flowers,
pendent, smooth as pearls.

Without leaves or roots
ghost pipe depends on the underground mycorrhizal mat
that links its flower to fir and fungus.

Sprayed from pods in summer heat
or released to the wind,
carried by birds, buried by squirrels,
seeds cross lines.
How many years after the clearcut
did it take for the first Douglas fir to sprout?
When did the cedars take root?
Year by year the forest grew.
And now, seventy years later,
in the deep shade of the thickets,
hemlock seedlings unfold.

Each spring the Swainson's thrush returns
and once again
the plaintive song filters
through the forest.
The wood warblers, too,
come and go, filling the willows
with their soft piping.

The Elk River, north fork and south,
samples the whole watershed,
carrying rock,
creek by creek, gravel bar
to gravel bar, from Copper Mountain
to the Pacific Ocean.

Slide Creek, Lost Creek, Panther Creek,
Sunshine, Slate, Bald Mountain, Anvil—
creeks named and unnamed on the map
flow into the river, their rocks
picked up in floods, whirled downriver,
dropped, rolled, sanded, cracked, and lifted again,
and packed in mosaics on gravel bars

miles from their origins—
grey black brown green red blue purple—
dappled, speckled, mottled,
and shining like jewels when it rains.

A Pacific wren knows nothing of a bearing tree
or the monument set in 1992,
township, range, and section carefully etched.
Keyed to a tangle of thimble berry,
salmon berry, and vine maple,
and to the nest woven into the roots of a fallen tree,
a wren follows the song of a creek,
winding through the forest,
crossing boundaries from public
to private to protected land.

IV. Keystone

A wedge-shaped stone
at the top of an arch
locking all the other stones in place;

a foundation;

one hundred and sixty-three acres of protected land:
the first in a bridge from the Pacific Ocean
to the Grassy Knob Wilderness.

What will keep this piece of land safe?
What will keep it wild?

Follow the contours of the land
to the far northeast corner,
elevation 1240 feet,
where the Keystone tops a ridge
and tilts into the Rock Creek drainage.

Here, a grove of old growth Douglas fir survives.

Listen to the pattering of needles,
the tick tick tick of cone seeds dropping,
a twig snapping,
the wind in the tips of the firs,
a raven, a jay, a hawk,
the chatter of a chickaree.

Can we keep our promise?

The trees of the Keystone want nothing but time.

Photo: Drift on the Elk River

Nesika Beach Preserve

This stunning preserve situated on the coastal bluffs of the Pacific Ocean was transferred to Wild Rivers Land Trust from the Nature Conservancy in 2020. The 100 acre preserve contains Sitka Spruce, Grand Fir forests and rare plants providing a full range of conservation ecosystems that links mountainous summits to Pacific seastacks. Nesika is a prime example of cooperative landowners caring for the lands where they live while having the support and guidance of our staff.

Photo (above): Nesika Ocean View
Photo (opposite): Camp Myrtlewood Footbridge

Camp Myrtlewood

The Camp's outdoor forest environment is a prime hiking spot and shining example of a Working Lands Conservation Easement. Camp Myrtlewood is enjoyed by more than 2000 visitors each year serving as a children's camp and adult retreat on 160 acres of forests, streams and meadows. The connecting thread between healthy forests and healthy people is shared by all who experience this glorious location. Camp Myrtlewood showcases the ability of hardworking land stewards who provide people from all walks of life an opportunity to get outdoors and interact with nature.

Photo (above): Light Through Trees at Nesika
Photo (below): Camp Myrtlewood Cove Creek Falls

Bagley Creek 2022:
From Mill to Salmon Recovery

We are excited to announce an upcoming milestone on a project we have been working on quietly for the past several years. An inconspicuous turn in the road about three miles upriver on Elk River Road is the location of a former plywood mill—the Western States Plywood Co-op which operated from the 1950s to the 1970s. During that time the mill provided a boost to the local economy, hiring 120 employees and tripling the population of Port Orford. Eventually, economic conditions forced the small mill to close, but the legacy of the mill is still visible on the property in the two ponds that were created to float logs for the mill and store water in the case of a fire.

As a resident of Port Orford, environmental advocate, plus a staff member at Wild Rivers Land Trust, I am incredibly proud and thrilled at the clean-up efforts and restoration underway. The thought of salmon returning to their native spawning grounds along the Wild & Scenic Elk River absolutely warms my heart!
—Pamela Berndt

The dams and spillways that artificially created these two ponds were critical to the operation of the mill. However, they prevent Coho salmon from passing through this area of Bagley Creek and accessing over a mile of upstream spawning habitat. Given that Coho salmon are now endangered and the barriers at the former mill site represent some of the last remaining artificial fish passage barriers in the entire Elk River watershed, WRLT has been working with our partners at the Curry Watersheds Partnership to imagine what comes next for the former Western States Plywood Co-op property. Removing these barriers was identified as a priority in the Elk River Strategic Action Plan for Coho Salmon Recovery.

Unfortunately, contamination is another legacy left behind by the operation of the mill. Several chemicals have been identified in the soils on the property—some of the most troubling are dioxins and furans which are associated with burning treated wood or plastics. These chemicals bind to fat and "bioaccumulate"—meaning they can become concentrated up the food chain as contaminated prey are eaten by predators. These chemicals are associated with many different types of human health problems depending on the exposure.

We are working with the Oregon Department of Environmental Quality and the Environmental Protection Agency on cleaning up this site simultaneously with restoring fish passage on Bagley Creek. As we continue to make progress on this first-of-its-kind project for WRLT, we will keep our community informed and hope this marks the beginning of renewed health for our rivers and habitats on the southern Oregon coast.

Photo: Old Mill on Bagley Creek

PALOUSE-CLEARWATER ENVIRONMENTAL INSTITUTE

Idaho
Washington

The mission of the Palouse-Clearwater Environmental Institute (PCEI) is to increase citizen involvement in decisions that affect our region's environment. PCEI aims to encourage sustainable living, provide experiential learning, and offer opportunities for serving in our community, while actively protecting and restoring our natural resources. PCEI connects people, place, and community.

-Palouse Nature Center: Poet Stacy Boe Miller
-Rose Creek Nature Preserve: Poet Alexandra Teague

Palouse-Clearwater Environmental Institute

Palouse-Clearwater Environmental Institute (PCEI) believes environmental change starts with individual action. By engaging members of our community in locally-focused activities and educational opportunities, we provide resources necessary to make environmentally sound and economically viable decisions that promote a sustainable future.

Organizational goals:
- To promote the ecological health and social welfare of the Palouse-Clearwater region.
- To actively participate in the conservation, preservation, and restoration of environmentally sensitive lands, natural areas, and unique ecosystems.
- To provide opportunities for the free exchange of views in matters of concern to the public.
- To inform and educate the public on issues of importance to the sustainable future of the Palouse-Clearwater region thus promoting a well-informed, active, and concerned citizenry.

PCEI owns and manages two properties: the Palouse Nature Center and the Rose Creek Nature Preserve. Prior to the local understanding of colonialism and land ownership, these properties were known, used, and watched over by the Paluutspuu, Nimiipuu, and Schitsu'umsh People who are Indigenous people of this area. We honor the land itself and the people who have stewarded it throughout the generations. Through their example, we commit ourselves to honoring the earth.

Learn more about PCEI at pcei.org

Photo: Walking the Trails at the Palouse Nature Center

Palouse Nature Center

The Palouse Nature Center is a 26.2-acre preserve located within Moscow, Idaho city limits. The Nature Center provides a space for the community to enjoy the outdoors in every season without having to drive long distances.

People come to the Palouse Nature Center for many reasons: to take a walk on the trails, buy a native plant from our John Crock Learning Nursery, picnic on the lawn, bike on the pump track, attend Palouse Roots, our Nature School, or Nature Explorers, our afterschool camp, get creative in our Artist Studio, attend an event or gathering in our Nancy Taylor Pavilion or Thomas O. Brown Learning Greenhouse, charge their electric vehicle at our charging stations, play at our playground, pick fruit from our orchard, enjoy the ponds and wetlands...and so much more.

PCEI purchased the original 7.65-acre Palouse Nature Center site in 2004 and began making improvements such as creating walking trails, adding a universally-accessible pathway, installing outdoor art pieces, nurturing wetlands, and building new structures. PCEI purchased additional parcels, and in 2016, received a generous donation from a neighbor of 8.8 acres, bringing the Nature Center acreage to 26.2 acres of beautiful, preserved open space.

Photo: Native camas, rescued from a local highway expansion site,
blooms on the hillsides of the Palouse Nature Center

Let Beauty
by Stacy Boe Miller

The lone pair of bluebirds
got an early start this year.

I sing a small triumph
for four fledglings in the nest.

My voice crawls a ladder
of wind to the dark-haired boy

running through the yarrow. I saw him
yesterday, drawing teasel—a weed

crowding what belongs.
His teacher smiling

over his shoulder. Let's let beauty
live a little longer.

Photo: A summer day at the Palouse Nature Center

Watch
by Stacy Boe Miller

I held my breath the first time
I saw a barn swallow. Blue angel
on a wooden door. I followed her

to the bridge. A man told me once
he felt the same way

when he saw his first magpie. Of course,
we seek the fat lip of an orchid,

the shocking mix and match
of a western tanager,
but don't forget the dip and rise
of a swallow's busy flight,

the crisp belly
of a magpie, deep
night of his open wings.

Watch me! he calls,
and the magic is
that we do.

Prairie Smoke
by Stacy Boe Miller

There's a ridge we aren't allowed
to hike anymore. I used to go there
before divorce to see if my desires

were different above the ridge line.
The flowers—so good
that year. We crouched to inspect,
took pictures to remember in January,

what pink looks like,
how red can pop,

until *No Trespassing*
signs went up. So, I come where
I'm welcome and listen—

the small fierceness of bees,
a chickadee's stutter. This evening

the prairie smoke are little,
ladies just waking up.

I ask which way the wind is going
and they tilt their messy heads.

Rose Creek Nature Preserve

The Rose Creek Nature Preserve is a special place located 7.5 miles northwest of Pullman, Washington. The Rose Creek Nature Preserve is the best example of the distinct quaking aspen-black hawthorn-cow parsnip community type of its kind remaining in the endangered Palouse meadow steppe ecosystem. Visitors to the 22-acre preserve can walk the trails to enjoy the beautiful Rose Creek surrounded by a plant community of native bunchgrass species in the upland, a lush community of species such as Fendler's waterleaf, and purple trillium in the wet meadow.

PCEI managed the Preserve for The Nature Conservancy of Washington for three years, after which they transferred the title of the land to PCEI in December 2008. As the new owners of the Preserve, PCEI maintains the high standard of care and concern for the historical preserve. By 2015, PCEI received two generous donations totaling 10 acres, and including the original homestead, from Fred Hudson (son of George and Bess Hudson who made the original 12-acre donation to the Nature Conservancy). We are grateful to the Hudson family for their generosity and preservation of this beautiful native Palouse prairie.

Photo: Winter descends over the Rose Creek Nature Preserve
by Casey Lowder

The Uncultivated Sonnets
        Rose Creek, Washington
by Alexandra Teague

Prairie

For which the speech of England has no name,
for which the cow parsnip also calls in silence—
for which wind tangles between the hawthorn's
lichened-gold, like ribbons in a child's hair;
in which the ribs of a deer are a shipwreck—
neptunia prata: the grassland of water. Water-
leaf with its broad bright leaves submerging
earth that was snowdrift in green, surging spring
into the crooked quiet.
                        Flit of red-flecked red-
winged blackbird wing: ripple and rumple of prairie
for which the speech of cultivation has no name
but plow. For which the harrowing and straight line
make a flag of a field of a scatter of wildstreaked
iris, purple and white-dapple, catchfly and fescue bunching

as the creek crinkles by in the sprung spring
sunlight for which the speech can only say grosbeak
and warbler and chokecherry, borrowing wings
and soft mists of blooms with their still gold
eyes for what keeps drawing new beauties like doodles
on paper ripped from a notebook
                            then caught in an updraft til the shaggy
spirals unravel the way every teacher of every ruler-gridded
chalkboard's small green field fears, and the way birds dream of
for nest fluff—for which there is new need each spring as the dogwoods
stalk their flamey stalks of red: inextinguishable fires along the creekbed;
winter—like the hawthorn thicket—cut back just
enough for me to pass in the first March sun
as the prairie reprairies itself into the garden it was
before anyone planted it, into the lungfilling word of itself.

Two Stories of a Field

red-osier dogwood hawthorn waterleaf blue
elderberry fern-leafed desert parsley spreading
dogbane wood's rose arrowleaf balsam-root nettle-
leaf horsemint strawberry tapertip onion sego lily
yellowbell camas wildrye bittercherry chokecherry
serviceberry mountain sweet root wax currant big
huckleberry huckleberry bristly Nootka rose cow-
parsnip creeping Oregongrape large fruit desert
parsley mountain sweetroot northern mule ears red
raspberry quaking aspen catchfly fescue blanket
flower wheat wheat wheat wheat wheat wheat
wheat wheat wheat wheat wheat wheat wheat
wheat wheat wheat wheat wheat wheat wheat
wheat wheat wheat wheat wheat wheat wheat

Garden

To call it a garden does not have to mean
you planted the hawthorns and dogbane and fawn lily.
That there were names before these names
is a fact. That there were plants before names. In one story,
crushed serviceberries turn a lake to blue.
In another, the landscape is a game of chutes and ladders:
up the road to holiness on smooth, tilled rungs;
beware the mud-mucky slide down to hell or earthworms.
Each square a field where only vice or virtue grows.
A snake's tongue flicks vanity; a ladder leads to kindness.
But even snakes coil back on themselves. *Beware*
the tail that is not a tail, a different game might say. Poultice
and poison can come from a single root. *Red pitch*
gum from Ponderosa pine can cure snow blindness. Northern mule's ear

stems can be eaten like celery. In one story, I am a settler here
on a bridge in the cold spring sun, trying to unsettle
what this land could say: like the volunteers planting saplings.
Or George Hudson—zoologist who studied minute
musculatures of birds—helping hawthorns rethicket, tangling
what had been cleared and plowed and sprayed.
To call this a garden now might mean I'm standing on a bridge
between stories. In one, the swallows swoop into neat
hammered houses, and the air smells of creosote, the ridge's
wheat, the ancient, tended damp of creek.
In another, wild roses ward off ghosts. Give this field long
enough, and I believe it: roses brambling back
across the ghost-pale stalks. *These are not different stories at all,*
but one place, shadowed and whirring and rushing,
            a better story might say.

☼

N.B. "The Uncultivated Sonnets" quote William Cullen Bryant's "The Prairies" and
also draw from "The Palouse Prairie, a Vanishing Indigenous Peoples Garden" by
Cleve Davis, and other readings about Rose Creek, George Hudson, and the Palouse.

Photo: Crossing Rose Creek on the beautiful bridge at the
Rose Creek Nature Preserve

Photo: Rose Creek winds through the Rose Creek Nature Preserve

Photo (above): Beautiful sunsets are commonly seen at the Palouse
Nature Center
Photo (below): The originial, now endangered, Palouse Prairie ecosystem
of the Rose Creek Nature Preserve

PAYETTE LAND TRUST

Idaho

Payette Land Trust (PLT) is dedicated to conserving for future generations the scenic, agricultural, ranch, recreational, historic, and wildlife values of West Central Idaho.

The PLT believes in conserving the rural landscape of West Central Idaho for the benefit of our community and future generations.

- We promote a community ethic that values and conserves its working agricultural properties and timberlands in balance with thoughtful development.
- We envision dedicated areas of open access and connectivity encouraging people to take part in their environment.
- We believe in maintaining the region's pristine rivers, streams, meadows and lakes for present and future generations.

-The Huffman Property
-South Fork Ranch

Poet: CMarie Fuhrman

Payette Land Trust History

Almost thirty years ago, the inspiration for Payette Land Trust arose from a collaboration between a local attorney, dedicated local residents, and a retired physician, Dr. Phyllis Huffman. All had a passion to protect the uniqueness of the region, and through them community conservation took hold in West Central Idaho.

Noticing the growth in population, Dr. Huffman recognized that Idaho's cherished landscapes were at risk of development. She was committed to seeing the Huffman property stay open space and began discussions with PLT even before it was an officially recognized land trust.

At the same time, community members became concerned at seeing their area change and the small group sprang into action. PLT's founding members dedicated the new organization to protecting the unique agricultural character, vibrant wildlife populations and the incredible scenic beauty of Long Valley. Their drive for conservation evolved into the formation of PLT in late 1993.

In the early years PLT had tremendous success, and by 2007 there were 11 easements in 4 different counties. 2008 brought a downturn in the economy, and the land trust began to suffer the repercussions from it. For close to 10 years PLT struggled to regain its momentum.

With help from the Land Trust Alliance, a new strategic plan, and a reinvigorated board, the trust entered a rebuilding stage and hired a part time executive director in 2017. The transition from an all-volunteer board to a paid staff member set PLT on a trajectory for success. Now PLT is a tireless advocate for private land conservation in the region.

In the last three years PLT has completed four conservation easements, opened three miles of the Payette River to access for the public and has five agricultural easements in process.

With a flood of people from across the nation moving to its rural areas, Idaho is one of the fastest growing areas of the country. PLT has its hands full with new easements, public education, and partnerships to make sure the region retains the unique and wonderful lands which make up West Central Idaho.

PAYETTE LAND TRUST WORKING AREA

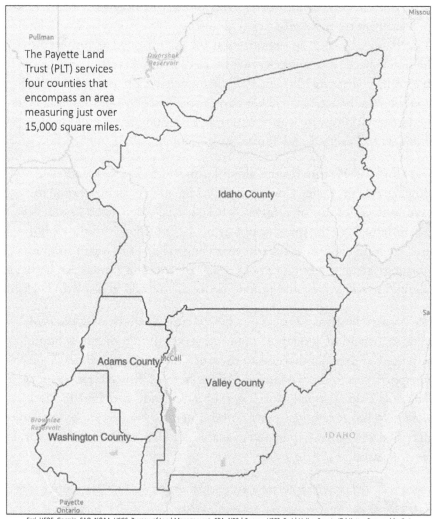

The Payette Land Trust (PLT) services four counties that encompass an area measuring just over 15,000 square miles.

Idaho County

Adams County

Valley County

Washington County

The Huffman Property

The story of PLT begins with a property, the Huffman Property, that helped to establish our organization. In 1991, Dr. Phyllis Huffman M.D., better known as "Phyd," entertained the idea of committing her property on Potter Lane to the idea of conservation. In a bequest, Phyd arranged for her property to be gifted to a land trust. The property was to be held in perpetuity by such an organization for the purpose of preserving the open space. It would take two more years for Payette Land Trust to gain its charter in 1993. In 1997, she finalized a trust in which PLT would be the beneficiary of her two properties. Phyd passed in 2002 and the Huffman property was transferred, becoming the second property endowed to Payette Land Trust.

The Huffman Pasture resides along Farm to Market Road, an ever-growing area of Valley County, Idaho. The 70-acre field is home to a fantastic collection of erratics. These glacially deposited boulders give testament to the massive power of ice, which carved through the area, creating majestic lakes and sprawling valleys. On warm summer mornings, from the boulder field, a pair of Sandhill Cranes can be heard calling for their young and reminding us of the wild in our own backyard.

The 35-acre Huffman Forest quietly conceals a stretch of Lake Fork creek in a stand of lodgepole pine and aspen. While sharing a boundary with the Carefree subdivision to the west, the property's character transports you to the wilderness. As the herd of fifty elk rise from their beds on a cold crisp fall morning, they agree and say thanks to Phyd. Thanks to her forethought and commitment to conservation, they know this place will remain open and available for all time, even as the world develops around it.

Like winds and sunsets, wild things were taken for granted until progress began to do away with them. Now we face the question whether a still higher 'standard of living' is worth its cost in things natural, wild and free.
— Aldo Leopold, *A Sand County Almanac*

Through the unselfish embodiment of Leopold's words, Phyd's commitment to the idea of conservation back in 1991 helped cultivate the organization which would become today's Payette Land Trust.

Poems by CMarie Fuhrman

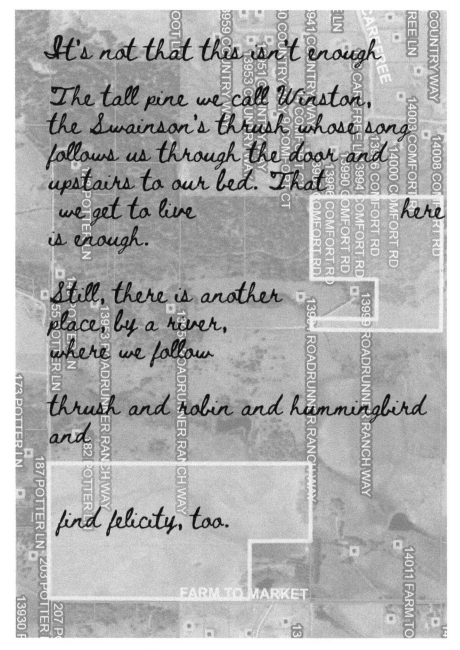

It's not that this isn't enough

The tall pine we call Winston,
the Swainson's thrush whose song
follows us through the door and
upstairs to our bed. That
 we get to live   here
is enough.

Still, there is another
place, by a river,
where we follow

thrush and robin and hummingbird
and

find felicity, too.

Said Thatching Ant

This hill you climb
carrying a piece of detritus
at a time, is the hill you make.

Sometimes it's hard to see
what you're capable of
when you're small
and already standing atop it.

Photo: Ant Hill on Payette Riverwalk Property by Craig Utter

Basic Facts of Existence

Some evenings, when we lose ourselves
to the untrail, find anthills that outweigh
us, and rivers of battered silver—

when above all else we are seduced
by elk bugle, cajoled by aspen rain,
we forget, for an indifferent moment—

this too shall pass.

Photo: South Fork Mules in Snow by Wes Gregory

Photos (above & below): two views of Huffman boulders by Craig Utter

Photo: Huffman Forest by Craig Utter

South Fork Ranch

The South Fork Ranch is located in some of the most rugged and beautiful country in West Central Idaho. The remote 100-acre property, accessible only by plane or snowmobile in the winter, is situated alongside the South Fork of the Salmon River, sharing a mile of river frontage, and surrounded by the Payette National Forest and the Frank Church River of No Return Wilderness.

The South Fork Ranch, previously known as Hettinger Ranch, has been home to people for thousands of years. The first evidence of inhabitants in this area date back over 10,000 years. Shallow impressions of house pits and art remain on or near the property and descendants of the early occupants still come to the river to fish, gather, and celebrate.

White settlers began to homestead the area in the late 1870s and early 1880s when the first claim was filed. Unsuccessful for mining, the land became the site for a would-be log mill. In 1958 the mill was erected on the shore of the river, but a permit for logging was never issued, so the mill never became operational and was partially dismantled in 1974. The remnants of the mill were fully removed in 2019, 61 years after construction by the Hansberger family.

In 2020, to conserve the heritage of this iconic riverfront property, a perpetual conservation easement was placed on the property through a partnership with Payette Land Trust.The Hansberger's, noting not only the cultural, historical, agricultural and aesthetic value of the land, work diligently to conserve the heritage of the land. Through careful ecological restoration to long term conservation planning, the South Fork Ranch will remain a place where culture, beauty, and heritage will live on.

The Land unites us with [our ancestors] across time, keeping our culture alive . . . .
We live in the place our ancestors called home before the great pyramids of Egypt were
built.

—Nez Perce Tribal Executive Committee

www.npshistory.com/publications/nepe/index.htm

Photo (above): South Fork Ranch Gate by Rob Lloyd
Photo (below): North Fork Payette River by Craig Utter

Poems for South Fork Ranch
by CMarie Fuhrman

There is a meadow in the imagination.
It is filled with long grass.
Each blade is a memory
and each root, a thought. At the edge

of this meadow is a forest.
And now you
must decide. Will you leave this meadow
and enter the forest, or stay where you're certain
the rain and sun will find you.

Photo (above): South Fork Ranch by Rob Lloyd
Photo (opposite): South Fork Salmon River by Rob Lloyd

These Flowers, This River (Perhaps I Could Stay)

Hettinger Ranch, July 2021

These wildflowers are a celebration of water to soil and leaf to light, and this year they are heavy on green stems. In the evening light, they are twice their midday brightness. A bee lands and dusts her legs in gold. These flowers are women lazing on the back porches of houses where good work has been done, meals served, the kitchen sink clean, the towel drying on an over door. They are children smiling at what they don't yet have names for, stars, birdsong, rabbits sideways hop into tall grass. They are scarves of red and blue, yellow and white, hanging from fenceposts and clotheslines.

Were I to have more than one self, I would leave her at this river. I would gather my skirts around my knees, leave my sandals on the shore and sit on the lichened-covered rock that graces its bank. The water is not deep here. The stones on the bottom are smooth with time. Smooth with current and an epoch of seasons that have washed over and rolled them. Bare feet can find footing on and between them; erosion, too, can be a kindness. And where moss grows, my soles find another softness. I would lie my body back, as I have so many streams before, and let the water have its way with my hair. Perhaps I could stay until the season smooths me.

RELEASE

Trust

Salmon

Trust in

Salmon

the Salmon

peoples. In

dreams

of   Salmon

in

river

inspiring

place.

the vision of

land

.

naming it

home for

beauty

the land

has been dismantled . Now,

hear the words

"I knew a mountainside and

a star- summer sky that we

shall

have trust."

Trust the river .

"The potential

. No

alteration

spread big horn

sheep."

Trust works in Idaho, and

in landscape for

generations.

hold land.

learn

trust.

Photo (above): The Porphyry Fire by Wes Gregory
Photo (below): Hotshot Firefighting Crew with Mule by Wes Gregory

COLORADO WEST LAND TRUST

COLORADO WEST
LAND TRUST

Conserving Land. Connecting People.
Enriching Lives.

Colorado

The mission of Colorado West Land Trust is to protect and enhance agricultural land, wildlife habitat and scenic lands in western Colorado to benefit the community at large, enrich lives, provide opportunities for outdoor recreation, and ensure our connection to land for generations to come.

The trust was formed by a group of farmers from Palisade, CO in 1980. Seated around a kitchen table, they reviewed and signed the documents that would permanently protect their farms from development pressure. Trailblazers with a hardy resilience to setbacks, these Palisade farmers were among the first in the nation to successfully conserve agricultural land, and over the subsequent years, gained a reputation for working *alongside* farmers and ranchers across western Colorado. Now, with over 125,000 acres conserved in 6 counties (Delta, Gunnison, Mesa, Montrose, Ouray, and San Miguel), Colorado West Land Trust serves the farming and ranching community, preserves wildlife and riparian habitat, expands land and trails for recreationists, protects views and open space, and helps ensure the availability of locally sourced food.

-Potter Ranch (Ridgway, CO): Rosemerry Wahtola Trommer
-Three Sisters Park (Grand Junction, CO): Danny Rosen
-Avant Vineyards (Palisade, CO): Wendy Videlock
-Chateau Thimble Rock (Unaweep Canyon, CO): Ben Bentele

Potter Ranch

Real Time in the Uncompahgre River Valley
by Rosemerry Wahtola Trommer

An hour means nothing
to this rivulet
unbraided from the stream.
To the towering spruce,
what's a day?
What know these red cliffs
of a week? A month?
To the deep meadow,
what's a year?
But for those who give themselves over
to the wind-kissed field,
the quiver of grass,
the great rise of Mount Abrams
and the quieting,
for those who linger on this timeless land,
a moment could mean everything.

Photo: Potter Ranch

At the Potter Ranch
by Rosemerry Wahtola Trommer

On a day when the human world feels like a fist—
when it clenches and squeezes,
fierce and relentless—
I leave the four walls and sit
on an old fallen cottonwood tree,
long and silver and smooth.
There, in the center of a wide river valley,
I sit. And sit. And sit.
And the tall green grasses
and the graceful white yarrow don't refuse me.
And the murmur of waves
and the musk-yellow scent of sweet clover
replace any thoughts, save being here.
The ring of red mesas
with their vast crowns of spruce
form a vase great enough to hold it all—
and I am gathered into spaciousness
along with dark green sedges and white butterflies,
with the tantrums of brambles
and the tangled flight patterns
of thousands on thousands of dark tiny flies.
A flock of birds rise all at once from the river
and my heart and my eyes rise, too.
A long time passes before I am quiet enough
to hear the chorus in the willows,
the bright clicking of insect wings,
the silence that weaves through everything.
Then the flickers come close
and the dragonflies draw nearer in.
And I current. I cloud. I leaf. I wing.
I leave unwalled, un-selved.
The spaciousness comes with me.

Three Sisters Park

In the Dying Dog Desert
by Danny Rosen

stooped, hobbling, foaming at the snout; and with a tumorous eye

high noon with a smoke when a tsunami
                    of quiet
rolls over what nectar may be hidden
within a brittle leaf in a thin crevice
in the belly in the heart in the core
of our precambrian solid and still

movement is the stuff of humans
heading up single tracks in the salt wash
walking on white-crust on green mud
through a gap in the dakota sand
beaches frozen and frozen again
down into the morrison slanting
into the cretaceous sea

I imagine a festival
of dinosaurs

                  gathered by the river:
working together to stop all the killing
extolling the virtues of warmer blood
              quaffing designer suds
debating the odds of bigger floods

Above the Wanakah
by Danny Rosen

above the Wanakah big lizards roamed
the ground alight in the glow of midnight
the sacred gone secular walking spectacular
in the mesozoic our forebearers hid and ran
swam and disappeared in mud stuck in time
(a matter of passing importance)
as trails go by keep pedaling keep wondering
keep feeding your hunger to make
a difference as if the scene could be
anything but a sort of foam, a brief thin
ad infinitum a chance a dance with twinkle toes
in pointy shoes we walk the surface under the Moon
and Jupiter and Mars and Aldebaran
and many other stars

Trailhead Sign
by Danny Rosen

in case of pterodactyls:
rattle your skittles
&
toodle-loo

Look Out!
by Danny Rosen

look out on soft slopes from the middle of life
before civilization and gods were born
outlaws and wild dogs before us
a proto-rhinocerous walks across the trail
very rhino-saurian in the cephalopod swell
big and small thoughts salty and freshwater
fish airfish phish fans fish fins and shark teeth
in loose shale forming now in the gulfs
where we go whale watching and look out!
for rattlesnakes on the prowl for voles
and shrews—who have really come a long way
from the old swamp to be here in the desert

Photo: Three Sisters Open Space

Avant Vinyards

The Vineyard Known as Avant
by Wendy Videlock

The first day the poet made her way
to the vineyard known as Avant
she was greeted by a sun-drenched

and smiling grower, a lazy June wind,
the scent of a rare morning rain
and down below, where the waters lay

a nest filled with sandhill cranes.
The second day the poet made her way
to the vineyard known as Avant

she was offered the rare sight
of a traveling snowy egret, a patch
of wild asparagus, and a gentle-eyed doe.

On the third day the poet made her way
to the vineyard known as Avant
she went slow and incognito

as poets tend to do, and found herself alone
and moved to the bone—
taken by the suddenly feline nature of the fox,

the dragonfly reflected in cathedral glass,
and scores and scores and scores
of sweetly ripened Coral Stars.

Land Marks
by Wendy Videlock

Dancers and dabblers, sisters and brothers,
makers and gardeners and under-the-influence-
of-the-moon students of gratitude,

I come to you from the foot, from the base,
from the sands of a table-top mountain known to some
as Mesa Grande, to others as The Grand Mesa,

to others as the Gate to the Rockies
and to the ancient ones as Thunder Mountain,
Thigunawat, or Land of the Spirits Long Departed.

It's said that wisdom lies in places.

This red rock world was once an ancient seaway, has been known
by allosaurus, inoceramus, Ute, Hopi, bighorn, lion,
hummingbird, hawk — is shaped by column, terrace, butte,

bluff and blaze, is formed by the roan plateau, globe
mallow, basalt lava flow, greasewood, slick-rock, mancos shale,
juniper and sandstone. This place on earth is also marked

by human greed and cruelty, by broken creed and tragedy,
by western wind and sprinklings of recovery. Today
this valley as the place where the peach

and grape will grow, is known for its million dollar breeze,
is known as the confluence where the Gunny and Colorado
Rivers join and have fallen low.

It's said there are no love stories that aren't blessed
or cursed, star-crossed and for better or worse,
                              rooted in this earth.

We gather here together in this place, in this life, in this world
to *endure*, as William Blake would say, *the beams of love,*
to deepen our knowing of currency and cultivation,

of language and of cessation, of story and of invocation, and
of time, with its vanishings and its traces and its wisdom
                              which is said, lies in places.

Unless you see a thing in the light of love you don't see it at all.

— *Kathleen Raine*

Listening Between the Lines
by Wendy Videlock

It takes a certain kind of hopeful soul
with a name like Diane
to plant wisteria on this kind of land.

It takes a certain kind of crazy soul
with a name like Neil
to grow grapes in high desert climes.

It takes a certain kind of love
to learn the alchemy of wine,
to learn the art

of raising the peach
on twenty acres of dirt — dirt
that's filled with alkaline.

All the world, it's said,
in a grain of sand,
in a glass of wine.

Here on the Western Slope
not a lot grows
but rabbit brush and cowboy's delight,

cottonwood and yucca, pinion
and juniper pine.
From the crazy to the sublime,

from the sugar beet to the stone fruit,
a confluence of rivers has come
to sing agriculture tunes.
When the grapes are in full bloom
there's nothing like it —
a headful of that scent will wake
you up this time of year, says Neil,
who coasts over to us

in a golf cart, fresh from the annual
Blue Grass Fest just down the hill.
One gets the feeling he rarely sits still.
Viticulture, he says, is a communal affair.
We never could've done this

without the help of our neighbors
and fellow growers— even still, the grower
has no reason not to grow — it's a passion,
it's a joy, it's a sacrifice —it's a Western
Colorado kind of roll of the dice.

Photo (above): Avant Vinyards
Photo (below): Driggs Mansion Thimble Rock

Chateau Thimble Rock

Driggs?
By Ben Bentele

☼

Who speaks to the monsoons within you?
☼

1
Remember that smell ?-

After a downpour on the Dobes -

& a killdeer flushes
before the flies find you

& the air is a twilight noon?-

Or do you?
Driggs?

What is it
you remember?

Could you tell me - who put thimble berries below thimble rock?
Or who thumped through this thalweg to build a home?

It is no coincidence
When star-silk & moonlights align

So
Tell me
Driggs

Do
Tell
☼

If I squint
I remember a canyon

... With two mouths ...

... 2 mouths
1 head ...

& a hand-full
of cactus.

2

If I asked you, in the tongues of Unaweep -
What language do you speak? *Tabeguache* -
                    Would you tell me
            West Sloper - where the sun lives? Or would you eat
                        wet roots along the Yampa?

Would you watch the turbid streams slacken
            Into a ruddy Uncompahgre
        Then settle down into the blue-green earth

                                    Sawatch
                                    Saguache
                                    saghwa-chị

            For do we weep
            For Hovenweep? -

Or have you forgotten that Deserted Valley? -

        - & Where
    are the people now

        Núu-chi?

        - & Where
    is their water?

| *Water* |
you are enough

You are never
ever
wasted

Breeze up my knees & blossom water

Or wash to sea no matter

.

You are water

..

We are water

...

| *You are* |

| *Water* |

...

Will there come a time
When we weep

When we weep & yell
& yell & weep
& the ditch riders of our hearts come to dredge our tears ducts dry? -

There are no trout on this jury
No sleek salmon to say:

Don't muddy the water with
    your prior appropriations man - my tears are salty & You
               have no
              jurisdiction
               here.

3

Stray shafts of sunlight

Rough ashlar
Mortar & stone

Watch it & surely
when you look
through the arch
there will be a fawn
in the apricot

Surrender
to it

Let the fawn's light lick you

Then
tell me

If you also
Would not live here

《◊》

I've never known two firs to be foes…
Never seen a willow sell it's shadow to the ground…
Elm offers crow her branches without gold…

But what about you human?

An apple is enough

more
than enough

an apple & the scent of chamomile.

But you
What about you Human?

I know the hoofprints of goats
The colors of bustard's bellies
I know what the moon means
       in
         the desert's
           dreaming.

           I know death
           in the haulms
           of pleasure & berries
           in the mouth's embrace

     - When the starlings arrive -
     - When the partridges chatter -

        Where the Rhubarb grows,
        When the falcons falter

           These I know

           This I know:
        The sound of a quail's flutter.

But you
Human
What about you?

Whose home is home if houses do not last?

- Or -
- Is home -

Is home in the coming home?

In the fawnlight of early dawn

When a meadow's meadowlark harkens the day

Or the coal train hums bluely
Below mesa

Is it the first gold leaves
Or the last gold leaves
Of the long-leafed lancing willow

Or the pink
Of your cheek

& The brown
Of your hand

Relishing
In the scent
Of fresh, cool pasture
To return, & know
My neighbor cut her sweet clover

Well,
Driggs? –

Where should I live?

Where shall I build my buggy
& tear it down again?

I must learn like the hermit of the hemlocks

I am no desert daisy

Can garden my own garden
but can't say much on your petunias

Have stood tall
in the tall
of a dark forest -

listening
to the sway of silenc*e*

Listening

Driggs

Listening

as sandstone tumbles into sunset

《◊》

N.B. The portion in poem 3 within the guillemets come from my translation of
Water's Footfall
صدای پای آب
by Sohrab Sepehri —
سهراب سپهری
.... Lines 231-253 ...

DRIFTLESS AREA LAND CONSERVANCY

Wisconsin

The mission of Driftless Area Land Conservancy (DALC) is to maintain and enhance the health, diversity and beauty of Southwest Wisconsin's natural and agricultural landscape through permanent land protection and restoration, and improve people's lives by connecting them to the land and to each other.

We believe that protecting the natural world and engaging people in its vast wonder is one of the most important gifts that we can pass on to our children and the generations that follow. We strive to educate, engage and inspire people and facilitate their connection to the land and to each other. Through focused land protection and management and by providing opportunities for people to engage with and enjoy the outdoors, we can help protect and improve the Driftless Area for everyone, forever.

-Gary and Rosemarie Zimmer Agricultural Conservation Easement
-Morrison Prairie and Forest Preserve
-Sardeson Forest Preserve
                    Poet: Erin Schneider

What is the Driftless Area?

Many people think of the upper Midwest as flat. Wisconsin, Minnesota, Iowa, and Illinois were all ironed out by over a million years of glaciers scraping over them, depositing 'drift' like boulders, sand, silt, and clay as they melted. But in the heart of this region, there's a place the glaciers missed – what we now call the Driftless Area.

What is commonly referred to as the Driftless Area includes the hilly region of southwestern Wisconsin, southeastern Minnesota, northeastern Iowa, and northwestern Illinois. It spans about 24,000 square miles – an area the size of West Virginia. This region has a unique topography of rolling hills, wide plateaus above sandstone bluffs, and narrow valleys carved by coldwater streams. Geologically speaking, only southwest Wisconsin and northwestern Illinois are truly "driftless" – meaning the glaciers never touched them. The area west of the Mississippi River was covered by the first of three glacial events in this region, so from a geological perspective it is not strictly "driftless." However, the landscape, ecosystems, and human communities are similar, and all feel a part of a colloquial "Driftless Area." To learn more, visit: www.driftlessconservancy.org/what-is-the-driftless-area

The broader Driftless Area served as a refuge to plants and animals when thick ice sheets covered much of northern North America, and still harbors rare and fascinating species. Since European settlement, as much of the Midwest has been converted to agriculture and development, the steep, rocky slopes of the Driftless Area have become a modern-day haven for dwindling native species such as grassland birds. The region's clear, cold, spring-fed streams also provide phenomenal habitat for native trout, which are threatened by warming waters caused by climate change.

But the Driftless Area isn't just defined by lack of glacial deposits, geography, or ecosystems. It also has a long history as unique and valued place for human residents. Today, the Driftless Area is full of productive farms, groundbreaking architecture, local food systems, art communities, state parks, hiking trails, and people who love and steward the land.

For these reasons and many more, the Driftless Area is a special place.

Gary and Rosemarie Zimmer Agricultural Conservation Easement

In 2000, DALC was created to protect land in the Driftless Area of Wisconsin by holding conservation easements. Twenty-two years later, we now own four nature preserves and participate in a wide variety of partnerships, but easements remain our bread and butter. At the time of this writing, we hold close to fifty easements on nearly eight thousand acres of land in the Driftless. By the time you're reading this anthology, we hope both of those numbers will be substantially higher. As threats to the land rise, so does the demand for conservation easements, especially from farmers who have spent a lifetime stewarding their land. It's a joy and a privilege for DALC to help these landowners protect the places they love, forever.

My gratitude to Gary Zimmer for taking the time to orient me to the land he and his family tend to in Iowa County, where this poem emerged. There was just so much wonderment to behold in early July, the walnuts, the blackcaps, the oyster mushrooms, the elderflowers, the creek beds, the views! My heart and mind kept gravitating back toward the care and passion the Zimmers have for working with the soil and what can happen when you revive the life underneath. What if the million dollar view is held in the overlooked and overworked spaces of the Earth, yet we walk over it everyday without giving thought to what it is much less what it does? And what of the rye that toils in the soil, a common generalist, historic castaway grain of the poor in Eastern Europe and the Russian Steppes, a cover crop among many as farmers exhausted the Steppes from wheat. Yet the rye the Zimmers are growing is specific to distilling 'Driftless Whiskey' and is part of a local agricultural value chain being cultivated among Zimmer and neighbors in and around SW Wisconsin. I also wanted to highlight that agriculture can be part of a conservation easement's management goals and that both conservation and agriculture can bestow 'reciprocal blessings', reviving the soil and the spirit.

—Erin Schneider, July 2021

A Rye Revival
by Erin Schneider

He steps a Walnut's length outward
brushes the bees getting fat off the pollen dusting his sleeve,
slips into a strip of worn, tilthy, Dolomite, immerses hands
in silken soil, built by layers of cooling plant sweat,
and beholds the million dollar view.

Ceres stirs and takes a care.

Soon,
new life releases from the plow as
minerals and microbes stir the pedon of a soul.

and
with smooth seeds and a fervid spirit,
He walks the fields, tussles the backbones of a million undulating awns.
Ryes' cloistered caramel-light husks, bow and release—a panoply of
seeds—
possibilities that distill in Earth's casks.

Later,
Stirred warm with age
each sipped from one generation to the next—no lime needed,
Their thirsts' quenched and soils' sated,
baptized in the dead body of grass.

Photo: Milkweed by Jennifer Filipiak

Morrison Prairie and Forest Preserve

Although DALC does not usually purchase land, the Morrison Prairie and Forest Preserve is an extraordinary Driftless landscape that we were deeply inspired to protect. This scenic bluff property includes dry remnant prairie, oak woodlands and savanna, and mesic woodlands – a diversity of habitat that supports a number of rare species. From the top of the bluff, visitors can see a broad swath of the Lower Wisconsin River Valley to the north, as well as expansive views of the wooded hills to the south.

We acquired this property in a generous bargain sale from landowner Darrel Morrison, a distinguished landscape architect and retired professor known for designing prairie-inspired gardens using native plants. Darrel's thoughtful partnership will allow us to steward and share this gorgeous gem for many generations to come.

I admit, I had a tough time finding entry into this poem and I also got confused on this site visit i.e. I thought we would be exploring a short grass prairie remnant dappling the South facing bluffs—once a typical landscape in the Driftless and one that farmers would often burn to renew pasture for grazing animals. There are some really amazing old landscape maps and photographs you can research on-line from the library/WI Historical Society. Instead I roamed through cornfields, an abandoned sunflower patch on my way into upland woods. Where was the short grass prairie? I saw a lot of signs, but still absence. So I went back to an old familiar form—letter writing, in trying to puzzle through how you write about an absence or lingering remains and retool what was lost.

—Erin Schneider, August 2021

The Morrison Letters
by Erin Schneider

Dear Farmer,

I mean no disrespect, I understand that aging has not been kind.
I read the wrinkles and furrows left in the wake
of your plow, your joy.

I walk right up to It—the curves dredged out of once watery mouths.
I miss your smile, your recent departure, that only 1% of you remain.
How so? Your footprints are everywhere.

I see you left untended to,
I walk toward the trees, adjust to the abruptness.
I pass by your detritus
the machinery, scrapped through the woods.

I understand you barely scraped by, even with all the inputs, welled
unseen,
and so the Gulf widens. I long to clear the hypoxic spell you were under
after the war.
When did you stop burning in the hills? I could use your old fire, fueled
by the blackberries,
even they lost sight of your edge, tasteless.

Dear Grandma,

I wanted to tell you that I woke up in the woods with a seedbank on my
socks, but you were gone. I slept in an old hog wallow, or was I bedded
down with Deer? I dreamt you were next to me, like a poem spellbound
between the oyster mushrooms that lit up the ash. I felt your oaken hands
in the shadows, grasped the aspect of this silent wind.
I tasted the milkweed like you said I should when the ache of absence is
too much to Bear.
P.S. How do I reach the Farmer, before it's too late?

Dear Remnant,

I walked the woods thinking I saw you, but they were all false openings.
Somewhere I have faith these letters will find you, because I tucked them
in the seedheads and left it to the wind.
What can you do with 10 acres, when you once roamed 10 million? The
bobolink no longer visits, there's too many rusted red cedar thinking they
own the place, though their gated limbs only cover the surface. Where are
my manners, my condolences for your loss.
"What happened to the Farmer," you ask?
I don't know, they lost the fire, burned under pressure, left a cataclysm
of stagnation laid to waste in unmet yields, misplaced policy, monotony's
grip.

I came for renewal and you deeded me a few acres of short grass, a
satchel of seeds on unceded territory. What were you thinking?
P.S. What did you witness in the Farmer?

Dear Morrison,

My fingers trace the curves of siliques inside my satchel
—two little workbags of women—
I release the ghosts of Grandma's consulates,
their tufts of white, silky hairs,
and with radicles at the ready,
they stream-line into the mid-level jet,
and balm the remains of stubble.
I watch the drift, I want to go back to the wallow, to sleep with the
furbearers, eat oysters.
I feel eyes ablaze. I strike a match.

☼

Sardeson Forest Preserve

Though this is DALC's newest, smallest preserve, it already has a poignant history and a bounty of ecosystems to explore. This beautiful hillside came to DALC in 2016 from Roland Sardeson, long-time resident of the small, artistic community of Mineral Point. Roland was to many the embodiment of Mineral Point - he was creative, adventurous, and loved his community.

In the fall of 2016, Roland called DALC and asked that we visit him on his land. It is a stunning piece of the Driftless, with towering rock outcrops, prairie remnants, and views to the west overlooking a valley bottom with a sparkling, meandering stream.

During the visit with Roland, he mentioned that he was having some health challenges. Little did we know at the time, Roland was terminally ill and making plans for what to do with his land. Within weeks of our visit Roland passed away. He was facing his own mortality and yet had the vision and compassion to think beyond himself. Roland donated his 12-acre property to DALC. We're honored that he chose to entrust us with his land legacy.

☼

All photos of Sardeson Forest Preserve by Mark Hirsch

Outcrops
by Erin Schneider

I.
Out of bedrock, I catch a glimpse of its Spirit flit and light up the
sandstone,
Points of minerals scintillate under a soapstone sky.

Out of sediment, I admire the heft
that only water on rock can interpret.
Its body taking shape, flows in the veins,
of a century old oak root.
It treads light, not yet hardened,
So begins the outcrop of a creative life.

II.
And now you are of the ground traversing
Boulder fields where maples and masonry
anchor eternity.
Somewhere, a cave
where isotopes reveal the jut of your rocky existence
I try to make sense of this russet decay.

III.
I bent sky-ways
diving in with the intimacy of eroding stardust,
So others may climb, perch and dance,
Play with point of view,
see the scene by scene
And surface amongst deposits of change.

IV.
Now, titled in prayer, humbled by the river
Its ooze and outwash outstretched like alms, circle
and unspool sediments of a remnant sea.

I enter Its cool body, deposit prayers in passing
to the unidentified skulls and femurs
scattered along the trail.
I feel their last frost-filled breaths,
imagine a bridge for bones to merge
with the stratum of the stream.

With no tide to rest such weary words,
I pray for life's continuity.
Give me a sign, a vein to interpret, the weathering of it all.

A fish jumps, catches a water boatman under a mackerel sky.
It's a good day to sail
I pray for an animal way of death.

V.
And holy hot damn the river is suddenly something different
She wears its rivulets of wet satin, awash in the intimacy
of the eternal. Her veins, change to
feed roots, polish rocks, carve caves, move arrowheads,
keep vigil for the boneyards of trees caught unaware.

Oh how she loves the splash and release
The making of curves, the bending of boulders,
the warmth of being captured in moss.

She hears the whisper of leaves
float their secrets to the sea.
She deciphers the calls of nuthatches
reflects on their read of the sky.

This precious light, the brix of sun, enough-ness.
She could answer all the eddies in the backwaters,
missed the beavers companionship,
Damn, how it could house strangers, bring life to the party.

She would need to go underground and perch before springs
surface at the base of bluffs, always the bluffs,
for a point of view and a chance to risk exposure,

All things I wished to be
Bless this power to move with Earth.

☼

THE PRAIRIE ENTHUSIASTS

Wisconsin

Wide open prairies and oak savannas once covered the landscape of the Upper Midwest. Today only a tiny fraction of these fire-dependent ecosystems remain, harboring many specialized and endangered plants and animals in some of the rarest habitats on Earth. Our community of Prairie Enthusiasts strives to protect and manage these complex, beautiful natural areas and help others learn about their importance.

Prairie enthusiasts work with landowners, farmers, and other organizations to save these prairie and oak savanna remnants which have persisted on the land since before European settlement. We focus on remnants because they harbor nearly all of the components (including life-forms such a microbes and insects) that make up a prairie community. Our grassroots volunteers also plant and maintain native plantings. We share our knowledge, labor, and love of the land.

We work on our mission through chapters in Wisconsin, Minnesota, and Illinois.

A map of our chapters can be found at ThePrairieEnthusiasts.org

-Mounds View Grassland: Poet Michael Brandt

Mounds View Grassland

Mounds View Grassland is an over-800-acre preserve that encompasses
four separate The Prairie Enthusiasts units: A-Z Farm, the Hanley Farm
Prairie, Schurch-Thomson Prairie, and Shea Prairie.

Site Steward

Rich Henderson, 608-845-7065, tpe.rhenderson@tds.net

Access & Directions

The Mounds View Grassland preserve is located south of US Highway
18/151 between Barneveld and Blue Mounds, Wisconsin. The properties
are situated between County Highway F and Mounds View Rd.
Addresses are:

Schurch-Thomson Pr (8624 Reilly Rd, Barneveld)
Shea Pr (3095 Mounds View Road, Barneveld)
A to Z Farm (3200 Arneson Road, Barneveld)

Description & Significance

The preserve is significant for its remnant prairie vegetation and
associated rare insects, and as wildlife habitat at both local and state
levels, such as the Wisconsin-endangered/Federal Special Concern
Species regal fritillary butterfly (*Speyeria idalia*) as well as many declining
grassland bird species including bobolink, dickcissel, upland sandpiper,
and Bell's vireo. In fact, it may play a critical role in prairie ecosystem
conservation in Wisconsin, for it lies within the 95,000+ acre Military
Ridge Prairie Heritage Area (MRPHA). The MRPHA has been identified
as the highest priority for landscape-scale grassland protection and
management in Wisconsin by the Wisconsin Department of Natural
Resources and represents one of the best opportunities in the Midwest
to protect prairie remnants and area sensitive species. The agricultural
history of the area has helped keep the landscape much as it was when
the first settlers saw it and has made it possible for plants and animals like
grassland birds, which have disappeared in more developed parts of the
Midwest, to survive. The Mounds View Prairie complex is one of the

three most significant concentrations of prairie sod and grassland bird habitat within the MRPHA.

In addition to grassland plants, insects and birds, the site is home to many amphibian, reptilian and mammalian prairie species, including our state animal - the badger! Along with prairie and oak savanna habitats, the preserve has cold-water streams, springs, seeps, and wetlands that add much to its biological diversity.

The Prairie Enthusiasts' long-term goal for the Mounds View Grassland is to restore, as much as feasible, its original prairie, along with some limited oak savanna. It is also The Prairie Enthusiasts' intent to expand the preserve should opportunities arise.

The current cover on the 572-acre preserve (compiled prior to the acquisition of the Hanley Farm Prairie) is:

Planted prairie	33%
Non-native cool-season grass	22%
Active cropland	16%
Active cropland	9%
Woodland & brush	9%
Pastured remnant prairie sod	7%
Wetlands	3%

Plant List

Over 400 plant species can be found on Mounds View, nine of special concern, state or federally threatened, or endangered. The complete inventory can be found here: https://tinyurl.com/h4w2xuk3

Photo (next spread): Mounds View Grassland by Eric Preston

Natural history

Mounds View lies near the eastern edge of Wisconsin's driftless, or unglaciated, region. Its bedrock geology was formed 450-470 million years ago during the middle Ordovician period of the Paleozoic era. The Galena, Decorah and Platteville Formations remaining as dolomitic ridges rising 1150 feet above sea level surround the site, providing breathtaking panoramic views. The gently rolling hilltops of dolomite slope down to shallow valleys with the side slopes covered in St. Peter's sandstone. The excavations of recently constructed badger dens can be observed in the easily excavated sandy soils. The St. Peter Sandstone is underlain by dolomitic rocks of the Prairie du Chien Group, which are not observable at Mounds View.

The Galena and Platteville Ordovician formations contain more fossils than any other geologic strata in Wisconsin. While stromatolites and oolites are lacking, the environment at the time was very hospitable to a broad range of bottom-dwelling, shell-forming animals such as brachiopods, bryozoans, corals, clams, and crinoids.

Management

Limited restoration work was begun in 2000, but most has been started since 2007, after permanent protection began to occur. In addition to planting prairie vegetation, land has been cleared of dense trees and brush that had invaded the site over the previous 60 years. Some restoration of the cold-water streams and wetlands has been started.

The restoration and management work has been done by volunteers and interns, and aided by contractors paid for with grants from the US Fish & Wildlife Service, WI Department of Natural Resources, Wildlife Conservation Society, Paul E. Stry Foundation, Alliant Energy Foundation, and private donations.

Ongoing management efforts include clearing trees and shrubs, weed control, use of prescribed fire, and planting of prairie seeds. There is still much to do, and it will take many decades to even begin to approach what the original ecosystems were like.

Perspective
by Michael Brandt

grassland is what people call it
the evocation of a broad terrestrial sea.
indeed, a person standing amidst its opulent waves
can imagine them coursing to the farthest horizon
unimpeded, unclaimed
making folly of boundaries drawn
from notions of necessity.

a meadowlark sees it differently.
the view from above
is not of a boundless uniformity, but
a patchwork of textures and colors
grasses to be sure, but woodlands too
and wetlands and even cultivated fields.
for the lark, these join to form an island
distinct in its integrity
a welcoming refuge in which to go about
the serious business of one's measured life.

come autumn, a goose will cross this very sky.
its years-long chronicle
composed from even greater height
marks this place rather than an island
a luminous tile in a grand mosaic
a single element in a work of art
still very much in progress.

compelling as fireflies in twilight
other tiles lay shimmering in the sun
to the south beyond Nachusa
east as far as Midewin
west to the Flint Hills.

fostered by countless hands and backbones
they propagate

implacably reaching out toward one another
eclipsing the overburdened
replenishing beauty
bringing into focus a truth of the soul
that the essence of nature resides
in creation.

Hearts of Oak
by Michael Brandt

a visitor may not even notice them
yet is likely here because of them
that is, because of the way their presence
has made this scene possible.
while the tall grasses and resplendent spray of flowers
all but command attention,
alone or in small cohorts
modestly stand the oaks.

in southern Wisconsin, oak trees are
no more remarkable than clouds
or fish fries on a Friday night.
a fixture of forest canopies
ubiquitous in the blended flora
of parks and neighborhoods
they seem to be everywhere.
certain examples may be recognized as appealing
because of say, extraordinary size or shape
yet as individuals, most go unseen.

here, some oaks have ventured out from the woodlot
to take up residence in the open
bringing to their adopted domicile shade, nesting sites
and provender otherwise absent
stirring changes in soil chemistry and moisture content

inducing subtle divergences.
the luckiest of these colonists will live to oversee
establishment of a proprietary, organic whole
greater than the sum of forest and field.

a more visceral impression emerges –
something akin to that of pins speckling a corkboard.
as their purpose is to fasten photographs
and notes of importance,
this scattering of great trees holds in place
a precious fabric
woven from threads spun over millennia –
a fabric which might well be carried away
if not for its guardian anchors.
resolute, through drought and fire,
indifferent to the harshest of winters
as well as the vagaries of human intentions
these oaks maintain their holy grip
invite us to weigh that quiet service
and challenge ourselves to do so well.

☼

Remnant
by Michael Brandt

they say the sound
was like a fusillade of rifle shots
cold steel wrenching its way through
a tensioned mesh of ancient roots
pop, pop, pop........
the funereal salute of a vast community
in honor of its own passing.

tracking their sullen oxen
the sodbusters would etch, line by line
a new narrative across the land
a saga of entitlement and triumph
a promise of liberty and
measureless bounty.

they had their reasons though
for passing by this particular place
too steep, too rocky
too near more compliant terrain
too small to suffer over.
so as centuries turned
this humble swatch endured
inviolable, inconspicuous.

"the last shall be first"
prophesied the sodbusters' bible
and today this remnant of lost prairie
is an object of reverence
a mainstay for those seeking to redress
the heedlessness of the past.
detached as a nude in an artist's studio
it offers itself up to scrutiny
the model and the measurement
of the thing itself.

a successor is already growing.
soon it will engulf this and other stubborn ancestors
in a landscape flourishing and profuse
expansive, breath taking
yet as imaginary as any adorning a gallery wall.
for the genius of the prairie remnant will be proven
not by the seed it has laid upon the soil
or scattered to the wind
but by that it has sown among the fertile workings
of the human mind.

Photo: Mounds View Grassland by Eric Preston

SCARBOROUGH LAND TRUST

SCARBOROUGH LAND TRUST

Conserving land for people, for wildlife — *forever.*

Maine

Scarborough Land Trust conserves land for people, for wildlife – forever. With community support, we have conserved over 1,600 acres to date, including a 434-acre landmark farm in western Scarborough, lands along the renowned Scarborough Marsh, and the land and viewshed of the Winslow Homer Studio on Prouts Neck. We also have an initiative to protect the lands adjacent to the five rivers in Scarborough protecting watershed values and wildlife habitat.

Once land is protected, Scarborough Land Trust manages much of this property as public preserves, open dawn to dusk every day of the year. We build and maintain trail systems, manage invasive plant species and improve wildlife habitat. Our education programs help connect kids and adults to nature.

Scarborough Land Trust is a private, non-profit, community-based organization. We conserve land where natural and agricultural resources, scenic vistas and historical significance offer unique value to our community.

-Broadturn Farm: Poet Cathleen Miller
-Blue Point Preserve: Poet Claire Millikin
-Pleasant Hill Preserve: Poet Tammi J Truax

Broadturn Farm

Broadturn farm hosts open fields, woodlands, streams, and wetlands, providing habitat for many species of birds, as well as farmland that includes agricultural soils of statewide significance. Part of the Stroudwater watershed, Silver Brook and Fogg Brook flow through the property into the Stroudwater River, which opens into the Fore River and Casco Bay. This landmark farm in western Scarborough dates back to the 1800s and includes an old cemetery. SLT leases the farm buildings and part of the land to local farmers, John Bliss and Stacy Brenner, who live on the farm. They raise certified organic vegetables and field-grown flowers, and host farm weddings and other education programs.

Photo: Waterfall by Dan Kehlenbach

Poems for Broadturn Farm Preserve, Scarborough Maine
by Cathleen Miller

January, Sandi's Silver Brook

1.
Ice piles in colliding shards
just past the falls:
a landscape of shattering,
water nearly solid
but for the trickle bubbling below.

2.
This is the season of clenched hips:
my body attempts balance
on the slick cover of snow
remembering   forgetting
fearing the ground underfoot.

3.
Litter of turkey feathers on the ground
blown by wind   dangling from branches.
Someone feasted well last night.
Wan winter sun   whisper of beech
voices of chickadees in the distance.

February, Sandi's Silver Brook

Squeak of snow under boots.
Sun on my face says "remember spring."
Groundhog says "six more weeks."

March, Sandi's Silver Brook

"I have no use for March,"
she said with surprising vehemence.
But standing here   on the fresh snow
in the ferocious wind,
sun warming my cheeks,

        I cannot help but disagree.

March melts our edges   until we move
from a glimmering trickle   to a full-throated gurgle—
our bodies remembering fluidity—
singing praise to the light.

April, Sandi's Silver Brook

Winter has let loose its accumulation
a season of holding released with a roar.

All you can hear is water:
brook song drowning out
the voices of peepers and wood frogs.

We, too, are caught up in the carnal
shedding of layers.
You invite me to "make out"
on the bench next to the brook
and I laugh.

We imagine the cool touch
of water on skin
during the hot days to come.

You rhapsodize about the lush, green
forest of moss underfoot.
I reply, "Yes, I always want
to lay down on it."

May 8 Opening Day, Broadturn Farm

And then, they arrive:
Tulips and Ranunculus!
Trout Lily and Canada Mayflower!
bustle and din   side by side

All of us more alive,
weighted down with bumble bees

Our voices are more
gurgle than roar,
a fuzzy green unfurling
seeds planted into warm mud
robin hopping on the path

So much beginning!

June, Sandi's Silver Brook

We are three days from exuberant bird song at 4:30 a.m.
        and our longing is palpable through humid breaths.
We are three days from eating extravagant salads
        covered with nasturtiums and heart's ease pansies.
We are three days from summer
        and the air is green next to the quiet brook.
We walk more slowly than last month
        talking about how uneven ground helps build neuroplasticity.
We sit on the same bench next to the rocky bank
        and we are broken open, changed by a surgeon's hands.
We are tender, scars visible,
        your brain healing as the world fills up with flowers.
We exhale mossy sighs in the thicket of birch and maple
        and the water laps against our edges.

July 21 Maine Women's Lobby Fundraiser, Broadturn Farm

We sweat and circle in the barn.
We raise our glasses and our voices.
We stoke the fires in our guts.
We know what is at stake.
We move from lamentation to exclamation.
We have come here to protect what we love.
We have power that cannot be taken from us.

When the grief washes over me in waves,
when I am overwhelmed by the enormity of what we could lose,
I walk toward the peach sky, clouds gathering in the West.
I walk through fields of flowers pleading for rain.
I walk, wondering how it is possible to feel alone
surrounded by strawflowers and sunflowers,
amaranth and dahlias, bumblebees and honey bees,
dragonflies swooping across the sky, crickets chirping,
and the voices of women
speaking about the revolution of relationship,
how care can save us.

I suppress the sob rising in my chest,
feel my feet root into the soil below
and continue to walk toward the setting sun,
carrying the fire and the ache.

August, Sandi's Silver Brook

The air hangs on our skin.   We are slick with sweat.
Under the canopy of trees   we take shelter from the sun.

August is thick with insects:
dragonfly dips low capturing mosquitos
water skippers tread across the surface of the brook
a frog rests on a rock in the shimmering green liquid ripples waiting
We cross easily over the sandy banks

where water has barely flowed for months.
We allow the quiet to sink into our pores
a relief from the crackle of brown fields, heat emanating from the
ground.

We listen to the leaves quivering in the light breeze,
feel the summer's end approaching.

Photo: Frog by Abby Wilson

Blue Point Preserve

Blue Point Preserve includes 800 feet of frontage along Scarborough Marsh, the largest contiguous salt marsh in Maine. Prior to European settlement, the Sokokis people of the Abenaki Tribe might have foraged for shellfish in the type of sheltered tidal wetland that can be seen from the marsh viewpoint. Looking out from that same location as early as the 1600s, you might have seen people cutting channels in the wetland to control the tides and harvest salt marsh hay. More recently, there was a gravel pit created on the northern part of the property. Neighborhood children used to ice skate on the frozen bottom of the gravel pit where the cattails now thrive.

Photo: Marsh by Abby Wilson

Imagine Blue Point, Approaching
by Claire Millikin

Driving past Jaguar, Land Rover, Mercedes Benz dealerships,
hospice, donut shop, faded motel,
I imagine what blue might appear
on Blue Point. Pearl azure, vitreous aquamarine,
incantatory nearing green, violet's elegiac slip. The turn

down the point marked by shuttered dairy bar and changing air,
salt in the offing. The difference of marsh and swamp
I think is light's available arc. At last reach
salt marsh blue as washed plates,
paler than rain,

slipped grain by grain in salt
and long ungolden grasses. It's not yet spring.
Initiate to water, blue keeps arriving, estuary,
almost a kind of estrus, this curved sequential opening.
They say the Almouchiquois fished here,

and for thousands of years this blue was theirs
by breath, eyes, touch. This itch of land
that now accepts my passing human steps.
My point on Blue Point is to say what is blue.
What is this blue?

A mirror, a thirst, a charm against the evil eye,
the talisman Efthemia gave me before the birth.
Beyond luxury car dealerships, hospice, donut shop, motel, dairy bar,
the point of it all: nothing
but land sinking, this listening.

An aspen shoot lean as a yearling deer
breathes between land and water. What is this worship?
Psaltic-blue, a taste like psalm in the mouth,
iridium, not cobalt, blue point's
rising waters, bearing salt.

Salt Marsh Elegy
by Claire Millikin

I've been looking for a place to hold my homelessness.
Not a bed or a door with a lock, I own those now,
but a place that answers.

Blue light across flat braiding water
then sun opens a door along salt hay.
Eelgrass, cordgrass, paper-delicate,

wind flaking the light between blades.
Grass is of subtle nouns, of no country or everywhere.
Sunlight tips a sailboat's edge toward another shore,

white flag of acquiescence,
man's days are like the grass, the wind passes over.
No ibis, just insects' call and response.

They live here. I've been looking for a place
to hold my homelessness, not lie about it, not undo it,
just hold it. The whole sky sets

a Sunday kind of light, though it's not Sunday,
the sound of insects and emptiness, like everyone's done with prayers
and slower. I've been looking for a room

that's not human. Sky exile blue, deeper than the soul
which is only a conjurer's trick,
being made of words.

Ocean-caught sky tarping to horizon line,
the lost table of origins.
Insects' quick bright syllables,

prayers refined to scars.
A new wind arrives, Pentecostal
tugging at worn-out shore grass.

There's no vanishing point
but an entire vanishing world, fold
where land, water, sky flow

into the same line and I know it's drowning, salt marsh,
sinking into rising sea waters,
but clouds grow luminous,

as if Aunt Lou's farmhouse stood still, down south
before the barrier islands, that house that burned down
decades back from faulty wiring. Celestial wires

tie this sky to water. One willet rises, disappears.
New houses built up along the eastern shore encroach.
A man comes down the path,

I don't know him. We cast our human shadows,
lures, ephemera into your shallows.
A quickening breeze. I feel in my pocket for car keys.

Pleasant Hill Preserve

Open fields, woods, wetlands, wildlife, and headwaters of the Spurwink River can be found at Pleasant Hill Preserve. More than 100 bird species have been recorded, including barn swallows that make use of the old metal barn. The Preserve is part of a wildlife and wetlands corridor that reaches from the Rachel Carson National Wildlife Refuge to the Scarborough Marsh. The land has a long farming history, and the metal barn is a remnant of days gone by. Jerrerd Benjamin owned the property for 40 years and raised beef cattle and other animals here. Previous owners included the Robinson family, who established a farmhouse and brick barn on the northwest side of the property as early as 1826, and the Lund/Johnson family, who built a house and two barns in the early 1900's and farmed the southwest side of the property.

Photo (previous page): Pines by Abby Wilson
Photo (above): Barn by Abby Wilson
Photo (last page): Elm Close Up by Seth Hanson

Japanese Knotweeding
by Tammi J Truax

Many have the most beautiful names:
Starry Stonewort, Rugosa Rose,
Flowering Rush, Dame's Rocket,
Climbing Nightshade and
American Water Lotus.

Each bears the characteristics
Americans have always admired:
resolve, resiliency, tenacity,
ambition, and plain old pluck,
to go out and test their luck

at arriving to new places, uninvited.
For some, like the Japanese Knotweed,
no beating back or digging out will quell
its own installation to rule as
Supreme Emperor of the land.

We, humans, heavily armed
with loppers, spades, scythes,
stand back to swear and stare
in sweaty defeated disgust
at what the invasives
have done.

A PHP Found Poem
From the *PHP 2015 Natural Resources Inventory* created by FB
Environmental Associates (Bizzari, L., Costa, K., and Ryan, K. "Natural
Resources Inventory - Pleasant Hill Preserve." December 2015, pages
1-57.)
by Tammi J Truax

East of the intersection of Pleasant Hill Road and Fogg Road
in Scarborough, Maine lies Pleasant Hill Preserve,

initially a dairy farm, turned to vegetable growing, cabbages and lettuce,
Hans Lund fished for eels at the headwaters of the Spurwink River,
three generations of Robinsons used the property for hay for their
horses.

Paxton fine sandy loam, Biddeford mucky peat,
the effects of human activity on the property are inextricably linked
to the present day plant communities, recolonized forest,
ditched and drained over the years, decades of disturbance,
pockets of apple trees, hardwood saplings take advantage of the light.

A mosaic of interconnected palustrine, scrub-shrub wetlands,
an emergent marsh dominated by cattail, spring water flows,
suitable habitat for wood frogs and spotted salamanders.
A muskrat in the open water,
a raccoon skull in the oak-pine woodland.

The Happy Tree on Monty's Path
by Tammi J Truax

I found a tree
smiling at me.
The hand of man
or Mother Nature?
We couldn't tell,
couldn't decide -
Man is tricky,
but she is brilliant.
If they were to work
together, what wonders!?
I'm inclined to liken it
to an aberration of lichen
while trusting that
Monty had a huge
sense of humor.

For the Swallows
by Tammi J Truax

It's July, they've finished nesting,
the young will soon migrate with their parents,
following their mother's call and the 48° isotherm…

Only to return in the spring,
coming back to their barn,
their birth place, their birthright.

Adaptation to us and our farms
resulted in their need now
for manmade structures.

And we must forevermore provide…
Pleasant Hill Preserve is theirs.
In return ~ they will return each spring,

live in enviable egalitarian couplings,
repeatedly recycle their mud nests,
raise another squawking clutch,

perform their high speed aerial artistry,
add brilliant color to the endless greens,
devour millions and millions of insects,

and share the cheerful
song of the swallow.

The Emerson Elm
by Tammi J Truax

Get under and look up
at the Emerson Elm.
See how it forks and forks again,
and forks again, and forks again

and again. Always reaching,

breaching, wanting to do better,
be bigger, grow, expand,
manifesting its grand destiny,
while standing perfectly still
asking nothing save sustenance.

I know what it means to be
a solitary survivor tree.
Defying disease and all
manner of insult and injury.
Sticking around, holding my ground.

Arms open to symbiosis,
quietly ringing in the years,
thankful for every single sunrise,
even those that come creeping in,
cloaked in a cold wet fog.

THE GREAT MEADOWS CONSERVATION TRUST, INC.

Connecticut

The mission of the Great Meadows Conservation Trust, Inc. is to promote—for the benefit of the general public—the preservation of the Great Meadows and environs along the Connecticut River located generally within the towns of Wethersfield, Rocky Hill and Glastonbury; including the preservation of the rural landscape, the floodplain and water resources, marshland, swamps, woodland, farmland, open spaces, the plant and animal life therein, and unique historic and scenic sites.

-The Wood Parcel: Poet Margaret Gibson

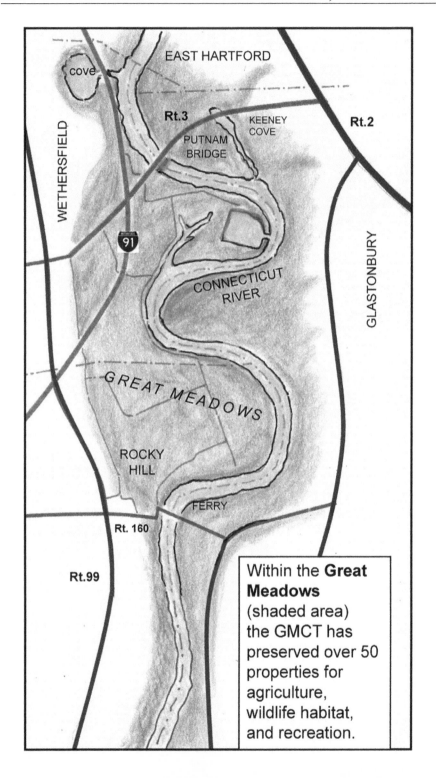

Within the **Great Meadows** (shaded area) the GMCT has preserved over 50 properties for agriculture, wildlife habitat, and recreation.

The Great Meadows Conservation Trust, Inc.

The Great Meadows Conservation Trust, Inc. has the following goals:
• To engage in the preservation of the Great Meadows and environs through responsible stewardship and management of the land the Trust owns and easements it holds.

• To engage in and promote the scientific study relating to the natural, cultural, and ecological values of the Great Meadows including its history, landscape, flora, fauna, recreational and flood control significance and to educate the public on these matters.

• To acquire, by gift, purchase, or otherwise, real or personal property of all kinds and interests, and to properly use such property and any net earnings exclusively for educational, scientific, charitable, agricultural, and conservation purposes of the Trust.

• To promote conservation efforts consistent with the mission of the Great Meadows Conservation Trust in partnership with landowners, state and town governments and other organizations

Map (opposite): The Great Meadows by Phil Lohman
Aerial Photo (above): The Great Meadows Looking North by Jack Jensen

History: 1968 - 2023

The Great Meadows Conservation Trust, Inc. was formed in 1968 in the pre-Earth Day period when there was no effective floodplain regulation. The Great Meadows had been seriously impacted by sand and gravel excavation, a former landfill, and highway construction. Fears of development were realized in the form of a race track proposal that would have diked a large area of the meadows in Wethersfield. Thanks to the Trust's first land acquisition of a small parcel at the entrance to the proposed race track, the threat to the meadows was defeated. For over 54 years the Trust has advocated for preserving the "oasis of green" in the Hartford metro area, acquiring 50 relatively small parcels "preserved in perpetuity" in fee ownership or easement, located throughout the Wethersfield, Glastonbury, and Rocky Hill meadows. Though they total only 200 acres of the 4500 acre flood plain, their strategic locations afford the Trust a powerful voice for the future.

Photo (opposite): Robins House 1936 by Edward Willard
Photo (above): Welcome to the Wood Parcel Trail by Jim Woodworth

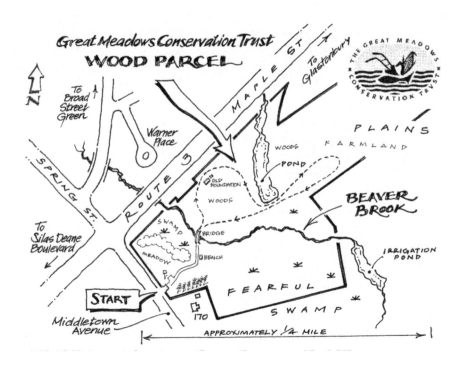

Wood Parcel Map by Phil Lohman

The Wood Parcel

The Wood parcel was purchased in 2000 from Sarah Wood, with assistance from Connecticut's Open Space and Watershed Land Acquisition Grant program. The Wood family, one of Wethersfield's few African-American families, purchased the 30-acre Robins farm in 1940 and built a modern house on the property when their 18th century house was removed for highway construction. As part of the Conservation and Public Recreation Easement and Agreement with the state, GMCT assures "that the protected property will be retained forever predominantly in its natural, scenic, forested, and/or open space condition, and [...] provide[s] opportunities for public recreation on the Protected Property."

The Wood parcel is GMCT's signature property. Other land holdings are located closer to the Connecticut River where there are no paved roads. Some are wetlands that can only be accessed in the dead of winter, on cross country skis, when the ground is frozen. GMCT leads "Brisk Winter Walks" in January and February to many of these parcels.

The Wood parcel, on the other hand, is within public view, and is easily accessed year round. Located at the intersection of Middletown Ave. and Rte. 3 in Wethersfield, there is parking available, and a well maintained trail with benches strategically placed for rest and reflection.

David Leff wrote about "…the value of natural places in thickly settled areas. They have a singular contemporary value and are often rich in both cultural as well as natural history." (personal communication with Tim Lewis 12/18/21) Margaret Gibson captured this best when she wrote, "If I'm still enough, in time present I sense time past and time future."

The Wood Parcel: Poetry
Margaret Gibson has captured the deep spirit of the Wood parcel. She is an internationally acclaimed poet who served as Connecticut's Poet Laureate (2019-2022). In her words, "Writing poetry is an act of attention and receptivity. You study whatever it is that strikes your attention—whether a scarlet tanager, river, field, or forest [...]. You take what's given into that part of the self that inquires, tests, embraces, and embodies. Outer and inner coalesce and fuse."

Ms. Gibson generously stepped in when poet David Leff, Connecticut poet and essayist who originally accepted the assignment to write poems for GMCT parcels, passed away unexpectedly. Leff's interest in the environment and "deep history" were a perfect fit for our preserved parcels on the edge of the Great Meadows.

Photo: Poet Margaret Gibson by Mara Lavitt

Meditation on a Food Plain Meadow Lit and Shadowed by Sun and
Cloud
by Margaret Gibson

1.
Time is a flood plain. A bone. A seed.

2.
If I'm still enough, in time present I sense time past and time future.

Skeow! yelps the green backed heron as it lifts from a limb
of the bitternut hickory,

and I translate the heron's monosyllable: *Now!*

3.
Now also, the sound of a tractor in the corn harvest.

Now, the crunch of my boot soles on the patchy gravel
and dirt trail that weaves past a slump of earth

where a house once in the 18th century was, before it was
razed to make way

for a highway—this whoosh on the edge of stillness.

4.
Just breathe.

5.
Whoever named it "Fearful Swamp"
was not a Wangunk.

They wove cattail mats, ate shoots and roots, fished
the deep river, brook, and cove.

They transformed plants into medicine.

6.
Time is the tractor that uncovers their bones while planting
seed corn, early summer.

7.
The photograph of an old, iconic American Elm in nearby Old
                                             Wethersfield
shows it to be 15 feet in diameter.

Now, as the ash trees die off, we plant American elms, disease resistant.

8.
Time is a cornfield. A green pond. A bench with a vista—

sedge grass and meadow swamp, bands of pale brown
and yellow and dusky green that whisper
                                         September,

9.
September, after a summer's hard drought kept all hands
filling five-gallon
plastic jugs

to water the new bare root plantings of tupelo, hackberry, tulip poplar—
bringing back the indigenous.

10.
Time is an emerald ash borer.

11.
In time past, Beaver Brook, considered by some settlers *inconvenient,*
was redirected.

It was common once, this draining of the flood plains for corn fields,
turf farms, suburbs, highways.

Where, where exactly, is remnant flood plain swamp and forest
now?

12.

If, with your whole body in sunlight and shadow you read the land,
you may
> sense a covenant

that links sycamore, migrant oriole, corn farmer, native pharmacist,
alluvial silts, arrowroot, and black willow

into one flooding of water wind sunlight earth.

Why would you want to alter that covenant?

13.

Last year's planting of young elms unfurls its leaves in time future,
making the present moment

steeper, greener.

But you must not ignore the doe, mangled alongside the concrete
traffic barrier,
> center lane, Route 3.

14.

Time past and time future abide
in time present
> beneath this canopy of towering sycamore,
burgeoning elm, swamp maple, ash.

15.

Time is a flood plain. A bone. A seed.

Photo: Green Heron by Jim Woodworth

Photo: Redtail Hawk Circles Over The Wood Parcel by Jim Woodworth

Photo (above): Fearful Swamp by Tim Lewis
Photo (below): Jared Christensen, 5th generation of the Anderson Farm
family, harrowing the corn field by Jim Woodworth

Photo: Boneset, an Eastern North American Perennial Native Herb
by Jim Woodworth

Beaver Brook Overlook by Phil Lohman

DARIEN LAND TRUST

Connecticut

The Darien Land Trust permanently preserves and restores open space, providing the community with environmentally rich habitats, scenic vistas, opportunities for educational experiences and the quiet enjoyment of nature.

The land trust works to preserve the natural, scenic, historical and recreational values of our community. The land trust is led by a board of trustees made up of residents of the town of Darien, along with an executive director. Its funding is derived from membership donations as well as public and private grants.

-Olson Woods
-Dunlap Woods
-Mather Meadows
        Poet: Holly Russell

Darien Land Trust

The Darien Land Trust is a member of the Land Trust Alliance (LTA), a national network of more than 1,700 community-based land trusts throughout the United States. The LTA is a powerful advocate and voice for conservation needs nationwide. Because we share a common environment, our personal health and the environmental well-being of our community are forever connected. The land trust protects our community by accepting gifts of open space and by acting as stewards of the land entrusted to us for perpetuity.

The Darien Land Trust provides stewardship for more than 220 acres that represent diverse natural environments, including upland forest at Dunlap Woods; woodlands at Cherry Lawn Trails, Olson Woods and Tokeneke Preserve; meadow habitat at Mather Meadows, Goodwives Meadow, Fox Run and Nearwater Lane; wetlands along Five Mile River and Valley Forge; tidal salt marshes at Holly Pond and Scott's Cove and a biodiverse suburban habitat using native plants at Waterbury Field.

Although many properties are too wet or fragile for pedestrian access, the Land Trust welcomes the public to explore three properties: Cherry Lawn Trails, Dunlap Woods, and Olson Woods. These properties have walking trails and areas for quiet contemplation to glimpse birds and other wildlife and enjoy the tranquility of nature.

Photo (opposite): Egret at Olson Woods by Nicole Rivard

Photo: The Meadows Buzz with Pollinators of All Varieties
by Elaine Lloyd

Conservation-Minded Landscaping

Conservation-minded landscaping benefits the environment. The land trust's approach to conservation landscaping is to protect and restore existing woodlands, meadows and marshlands by encouraging native plantings and reducing invasive plant species. When native species thrive, they attract pollinators such as birds, bees and butterflies that improve the environmental value of the land.

Numerous coastal properties of the Darien Land Trust follow the Atlantic Flyway of migrating birds. The waterfront location of Holly Pond, Scott's Cove and the Nearwater Lane Corridor provide a welcome place of refuge for birds on their journey, as well as protected habitat for native birds to nest and raise their young, including a variety of ducks, herons and egrets.

To enhance the coastal ecosystem of these properties, the land trust replants native tidal marsh grasses and plants. At coastal meadows, the habitat is continually restored by the planting of wildflowers and removal of invasive phragmites.

The land trust properties together create a green corridor that provides habitat for both migratory and native birds. The Darien Land Trust is grateful for contributions from photographers Laney Lloyd and Nicole Rivard, who so beautifully capture the wildlife on Land Trust properties, including a variety of native birds.

Olson Woods

This quiet and peaceful Nature Preserve lies adjacent to the Noroton River on the Stamford border. The river creates a pond where ducks, heron and other shore birds can be observed from the well-maintained walking trails.

In 2018, The land trust and the Connecticut Fund for the Environment's Save the Sound completed the Norton River Fishway, allowing the return of native alewives and blueback herring to the Noroton River Watershed after more than 50 years' absence.

The fishway provides clear spawning routes for these migratory fish who live in saltwater but return to freshwater to breed and can now access adjacent rivers and ponds, including Olson Pond. River herring play an important role in the ecosystem, both as food for predator species and as filter feeders, cleaning our waters. By periodically restocking Olson Pond with herring, the land trust continually helps protect this native species and improves the environmental value of the preserve.

Olson Woods, Spring
by Holly Russell

Silver bend of the Noroton River
capturing sky and
the dance of the trees
summons schools of alewife and
blueback herring who
flash in its depths to breed.

Photo (above): Wintery Shores at Olson Woods Pond by Nicole Rivard
Photo (opposite): Mallards are Frequently Sighted on Olson Pond
by Elaine Lloyd

Dunlap Woods

The trails at Dunlap Woods, a 22-acre nature preserve whose trails are linked with the town's 28-acre Selleck's Woods, are open to the public for recreational use. Dunlap Woods features a protected native plant garden, a vernal pond, a seven-acre lake and three bridges along its marked trails. An annual seasonal exhibition features wooden reproductions of birds of prey, native birds and mammals hidden in the rocks and trees. The stewards of the land trust maintain marked trails for walking in the woods.

There are seven ecosystems within Dunlap Woods and informational charts along the way educate visitors about their environmental value and diverse habitats. These ecosystems, which include woodlands, open fields, and wetlands with marsh areas make Dunlap Woods a sanctuary for wildlife. Visitors may see birds of prey soaring overhead, swans gliding past at Dunlap Lake, or woodchucks scurrying along the trail.

Photo: Fairy House Entrance at Dunlap Woods by Elaine Lloyd

Quiet World
A poem for Dunlap Woods
by Holly Russell

Leaves shelter the floor of hills and wetlands
caretakers of life on an infinite scale.
Brush piles house creatures.
A pool bubbles with tadpoles.
Swans and mallards skim the lake,
floating through the whistle of a train rushing by.

We forget to hurry in this place.
We take our time.
It's ours in abundance,
at least, that's what it seems.

Only the fairies might question the
lack
of urgency
whisking behind doors at the base of the trees
so that we see only shadows
of branch and foliage
falling over the trail when we pass.

The Land Trust Invites the Community to Adventure Day at Dunlap and Selleck's Woods

The Darien Land Trust in partnership with the Friends of Selleck's Woods and Darien Parks & Recreation hosts an annual Adventure Day with educational activities and interactive experiences at the Dunlap trails and lakefront for members of the community. Children are filled with wonder as they explore and participate in activities such as live encounters with small mammals, reptiles and amphibians; ziplining and crossing a rope bridge at Adventureland; identifying birds and learning about bird and bat habitats at an exhibition table; and contributing to a community art project.

Photo: A Friendly Mammal Encounter by Elaine Lloyd

Photo (above): Darien Land Trust Poet Holly Russell at Mather Meadows
by Amy Sarbinowski
Photo (below): Bridge at Dunlap Wood by Elaine Lloyd

Mather Meadows

Over the last two decades, the Darien Land Trust helped save Mather
Meadows, a 10-acre property, with funds from the state, town and private
donations. These magnificent meadows are maintained as part of the
disappearing grassland habitat in Connecticut. The land trust continually
adds more plant diversity to maximize the environmental value of
the meadows. By increasing the variety of native plants over time, the
meadows are able to support a broader range of birds, butterflies and
other pollinators. The land trust strives to limit invasive plants, which
allows native plants to go through their entire life cycle, producing seeds
and nectar for insects, the most critical food for the bird population.

In addition to a wide variety of native plantings, blue bird boxes and
bee apiaries have been added to Mather Meadows as part of an ongoing
effort to create an oasis of biological activity. Bees are carefully tended
from early spring to late fall and produce anywhere from 30 to 60 pounds
of honey per hive.

A recent addition of land in 2021 increases a valuable habitat that
supports a wide variety of birds and other species that depend on these
ecosystems to live.

Open meadows are used by migrating bird species along the Atlantic
Flyway as a place of refuge. The meadows are also used by the Monarch
butterflies as they stop to feed on the abundant nectar sources on their
return migration to Mexico each fall.

Adjacent to Mather Meadows is the Mather Homestead, operated by the
Mather Homestead Foundation. The homestead is the preserved home
of Stephen Mather, the first Director of the National Parks Service.
The value of preserving land was Mather's life work. He expanded the
National Parks and started the Ranger Program to educate people about
the relevance and value of the landscapes of our national parks.

Photo (opposite): Pollinator Plants at Mather Meadows by Elaine Lloyd

In The Heart of Mather Meadows
by Holly Russell

Four corners of history
resolve in this tapestry
where grapevines run wild,
and maple trees glow crimson in the fall.

A crumbling wall holds in its stones
secrets we'll never know.

Bees sift pollen across from the homestead
humming past lives and deeds to the pulse of the earth
spinning on its axis
connecting with the stars, constant and eternal.

And one generation slips into the next,
the ground here to catch us when we fall.

Partnering with Neighboring Land Trusts: Walk Your Land Trust Spring and Fall Series

Last spring, The Darien Land Trust partnered with the Norwalk Land Trust, New Canaan Land Trust and Stamford Land Conservation Trust to host Walk Your Land Trust Days, guided walks on selective properties that are offered to the membership of all four land trusts. The Darien Land Trust hosted a trail walk at Dunlap Woods, New Canaan Land Trust featured a nature walk at the Silvermine-Fowler Preserve, Norwalk Land Trust led a forest bathing walk at Farm Creek Preserve and Stamford Land Conservation Trust led an educational mushroom walk at Altschul Preserve.

In fall of 2022, Walk Your Land Trust days included a beekeeping and pollinator walk with the Darien Land Trust at Mather Meadows, a mushroom walk with the Stamford Land Conservation Trust at Altschul Preserve, a forest bathing walk with the Norwalk Land Trust at Farm Creek Preserve, a sculpture walk at the Silvermine-Fowler Preserve with the New Canaan Land Trust and a Nick Parisot memorial sunset trail walk with the Wilton Land Trust.

Photo: Hairy Woodpecker by Nicole Rivard

Photo: Dunlap Wood's Walking Trails in the Fall by Elaine Lloyd

Photo: Watchful Hawk by Nicole Rivard

MORRIS-JUMEL MANSION

New York

As one of the nation's foremost historic houses, Morris-Jumel Mansion strives to empower audiences to create relevant, contemporary connections to the building, its collections, the land, and its people, past and present. Through historic site tours, programs, and exhibitions, the museum serves as a cultural resource and destination for local communities and domestic and international visitors.

-Poets:
  -Michaeline Picaro
  -Lisa "Rubi G." Ventura
  -Anacaona Rocio Milagro
  -Naa Akua

N.B. Materials for this chapter come from the Morris-Jumel Mansion's "Living Landscape: Mapping Community Stories" project, funded by the National Endowment for the Humanities. The project team included Shiloh Holley, Angela Garcia, and Megan Byrnes.

Morris-Jumel Mansion

The Morris-Jumel Mansion and the surrounding 130 acres that comprised the Morris and Jumel estates was built on the ancestral homelands of the Munsee Lenape Nation in the northern part of "Mannahatta," meaning "island of many hills" or a "thicket where wood can be found to make bows." For centuries, this land and all of Lenapehoking has been a historic gathering and trading place for many diverse Indigenous peoples, some who continue to live, work and maintain kinship ties on the island.*

The building was constructed in 1765 for the Morris family, likely using enslaved laborers. The house would later serve as the headquarters for General George Washington and other military encampments before serving as a tavern and later the home to Eliza Jumel from 1810-1865. In 1904, two acres of the estate were donated to the City of New York to become a public park and museum.

Over the past century, the area immediately surrounding the neighborhood has become home to a diverse population of New Yorkers. In the early twentieth century, the area became a desirable neighborhood for the wealthy Black elite during the Harlem Renaissance. In the past six decades, first and second generation Dominican Americans have made this place their home, currently making up 44% of the surrounding population, according to the 2020 U.S. Census.

Given their history, the fifty modern city blocks that once encompassed the estate represent a microcosm of American history, weaving together the strands of migration, colonization, enslavement, urbanization, and the ever-changing meaning of American identity and citizenship.

---

* Indigenous names and interpretations by Nikole Pecore, Lenape-Munsee language teacher and translator, personal communication with Shiloh Holley, 9/21/22.

We are Philipse Indians
by Michaeline Picaro

"We are Philipse Indians," words swayed gently on wind through family history over time, echoing along my oscillating adolescent inquisitive mind. Elder knowledge ringing in ear, propelling chronicles clear across decades of unrecorded histories, spoken words which swirl like vortex, as neurons apprehensively capture the essence of their meaning.

Wappinger, Lenape, Ramapo, Wecquaesgeek, Philispe Minsi, Munsee, these words stumbled about my brain, I hear knowledge is power, but what is knowledge without explanation, simple motivation for musings are assumed.

History speaks in forked tongue causing words to crash on ears like marching band cymbals, jerking the veil of fabrications and heavy opinion, upward to reveal its deprived truths.

"Frederick Philipse inherits Indian woman with child and several Negro's men plus women," sale and purchase of enslaved people elegantly weaving his legacy like fine lace for heirs.

Amassed heirlooms doth Mary Philipse Morris acquire with lofty mansion tethered to sprawling land, when fog is lifted, and dew remains fated for erasure like Philipse Indian trails once traveled.

Spirits of Ramapough Lenape ancestors entombed in timeline and stuck in history pages as final judgement of parchment genocidal doom, we are alive with spirit of ancestors and teachings heart, we are still here; Philipse, Ramapo, Wickquaskeck, Wappinger, Lenape, Minsi, Munsee Indians.

Between Hell & Hearth
by Lisa "Rubi G." Ventura

Here
an ode to black
limbs that created
magic within infernos
enclosed by white walls.

Here
an honorarium
for cooks
and service crews
of well-off establishments.

Here
in remembrance
of domestic staff who *punched*
-in before dawn toiling
late into the night.

Here
squandering
priceless time cleaning,
polishing silverware
their lips would never touch.

Here
in recognition
of hired, borrowed,
or indentured labor, barely
earning four dollars a month.

Here
in the abyss
of eighteenth-century
cellars, where hearth
and servant pillows are cemented.

Hearth
as in the section of a furnace
where ore is exposed
to flame and meal prep arduously,
lengthy.

Hearth
as in heart and family
as in vital or creative centers,
where food and love
long to be manifested.

Hearth
as in a symbol of one's home

but who's hearth is it anyway? if
mistress-in-chief never engulfs
aflame in it

"*In a society where role models serve as sources of inspiration, it is in the best interest of Dominican children to learn about one of their own who contributed to the formation of the city that they, as many others, have inherited.*"

-Dr. Ramona Hernández, director, CUNY Dominican Studies Institute, "Juan Rodriguez and the Beginnings of New York City" in *The Dominican Studies Research Monograph Series* (NY: CUNY Dominican Studies Institute) p.9

A brief but worthy account of the Dominican American prototype (an acrostic)
by Lisa "Rubi G." Ventura

Jung Tobias
was a Dutch merchant ship that transported America's first
                                        Dominican to the
United States
in 1613. The ship's crew included a black or mulatto born
                                        in Saint Domingue.
Ancestry
indicates he was also the first man of African descent in Manhattan.

Naturally
strong-willed, resilient, and hardworking.

Refusing
to sail back to the Netherlands and demanding to stay by
                                        threatening to jump
Overboard
if forced to retreat. The captain agreed and left him   behind.

Dark-skinned,
free, and from Hispaniola, he was recognized as the only
                                        nonindigenous to
Reside
on the island for a notable amount of time--

Interpreting
or making connections between Inhabitants,

Garment
Merchants, and Explorers--

Unknowingly,
unifying Dominican and American cultures. Earning
                                        honorable mention as an
Entrepreneur
who promoted economic interactions for the wellbeing of
                                        all parties involved.
Zealously,
creating a bridge   between Las Americas   and the Diaspora.

Elegy for Truths Disappeared from History [Books]
by Lisa "Rubi G." Ventura

i.
atop Manhattan's second highest peak
sits a 1765 George-Palladian summer
residence exclusively designed for British
heir. A white house without much external
flair but with unmatched views
of Harlem
of Hudson Harbor, a fortress
for Colonel Roger and Mary Morris--
the largest human dealers of their time
legally conducting trafficking affairs, publicly
quenching a thirst for arrogant glamour
by building fortunes with bludgeoned money.

currency claiming, *"In God we Trust"*
but greed only trusts the green
hues on its Benjamin's
wealth only trusts its addiction
to power & thus tower
over highly pigmented Americans. this game
been rigged from the start. affluence
created the regimen. hence,
why law is always
on the side of treasury.
lest we not offend
our pledge of allegiance, but this
is the origin of America's mysteries. nightmares
recycle themselves repetitiously & superstitiously,
privilege comes to colonize
sacred ancestries. presently,
forevermore,
brown & black
communities--

The genesis of gentrification.

records proving, we stand upon consecrated
territory, whose maiden name is Lenapehoking. Fifty city blocks--
wrenched from indigenous hands
to satiate European business & pleasures
consisting of genocidal experimentations. in the name
of economical explorations. who couldn't live
prosperously? predator
& prey(ing) their way through
Algonquin-speaking nations. a country's
foundation landmarked
for its colonization efforts but not
for the lambs sacrificed
by brute British hands.

for five weeks,
Autumn of 1776, General George Washington
& his team encamped
in the second floor's octagonal room, plotting--
utilizing said vantage
point to this country's advantage.

ii.
in 1810, Stephen and Eliza Jumel
purchased the residence and its surrounding
acreages. later, Madam Jumel, a self-educated,
businesswoman and widow
twice over, made a name for herself by marrying
immigrant, but rich. only to be scorned
by New York's haughty elite. unfortunately, her scheme
didn't guarantee a seat with the likes of Regina George
and her dweebs-- madam wasn't born into greed.
free as bald eagles on dollar
bills, Eliza did not remarry and began
to summer in Saratoga Springs, crossing
paths with a free
[black] family, a free
family, a

family.
hiring them
[all] as staff
& daringly, claiming black offspring
as her kin. but still
treating them like property.

iii.
Anne Northup; mother, wife, cook
& not quite a widow,
but a beloved husband
& adoring father had gone missing--
Solomon Northup, farmer
& gifted musician was alienated
from his relatives by way
of trickery. lured, kidnapped, & drugged
into slavery. hauled from Saratoga Springs to Washington DC
to Louisiana and finally, New Orleans. for twelve years,
a slave. clearing cane to develop
land that would never be entrusted
to any of his kids: Margaret, Elizabeth, or Alonzo.
for a decade, burden
of proof was on him & amendments
per usual, were not
on his side. Typical narrative of [Black]
America
                                        the great.

iv.
(*epilogue*)

lest we never
forget there are two sides
to every quarter but underdogs
always foot the bill. and so,
this reverence & spot
light is reserved for the lives
that never mattered. for the flesh

that endured as souls
decayed--
loosing hope, strength,
& perhaps, the desire
to remain alive. doing so
anyway, while humbly serving
its enemy.

Art: View of the Harlem River with the Morris-Jumel Mansion on the left, illustrated before the construction of the Croton Aqueduct and High Bridge. Credit: Engraved by William James Bennett after Fayette Bartholomew Tower, Wiley & Putnam (Publisher), "View of the Jet at Harlem River," 1843, from *Illustrations of the Croton Aqueduct*, Courtesy of The Miriam and Ira D. Wallach Division of Art, Prints and Photographs: Print Collection, The New York Public Library

Mangoes on the Moon over Morris-Jumel Mansion NYC
by Anacaona Rocio Milagro

> *The land! Don't you feel it? Doesn't it make you want to go out*
> *and lift dead Indians tenderly from their graves, to steal from them—*
> *as if it must be clinging even to their corpses—some authenticity [...]*
> *—Williams Carlos Williams**

A mango tree planted at Morris-Jumel Mansion in New York City
will die. Mangoes cannot grow here. The climate's wrong   lacking
proper warmth   the sun   not strong enough   the New York frost
will eat it   barren   inside out.   This is law.

Morris-Jumel Mansion is dignified in its old-fashion patriotic pride.
The Daughters of the American Revolution   so honored   its rich
walls hugged our beloved founding fathers hailing Mount Morris a
historical landmark. Right here on the crowned sugar-coated hill of

Washington Heights. Born and raised down the block   this is my
home that I love   the only home I've ever known   I am American
vacant of this unadulterated nationalism—the root and fruit of this
Mansion   its settlers   of the die-hard   self-proclaimed   proud

red-blooded Americans   that I am not.

Pride   in the human heart   can only grow   in certain climates.
How does pride grow here?   In this cold.   On this soil.   How does
it not rot   with grief/   blood-clots/   with the starved demoralized
smallpox genocides/ the Indian Wars/ the African Holocaust? What

compartment in the human genome exists   big enough   strong
enough to suppress this knowledge? Grand larceny/ mass murder/
this Mansion erected on graves/ at what proximity do you displace
these crimes to give room for pure pride   to bloom   to flourish

unchallenged   in a human heart?   How does pride grow here?

Yet, I am confronted by it, touring the Mansion   confused by it

as I'm touring the Mansion   it is encased in glass in the Mansion.
Mango trees everywhere. Make it make sense. What Frankenstein
science could allow such pride to grow wild into jungles   ferment

get drunk   off all the life, liberty, and happiness that it wants
unchecked in a human heart? Can you grow mangoes on the moon
and not crack and decompose under the sheer dense freezing
cold suffocating darkness of it all?   We cannot change history

and   facts do not have alternatives. You, proud American, who can
house our evil past without pause in your human heart—does it hide
from you   do you mute it   drown it in pesticides   is it buried
out of sight   like the unmarked Lenape cemeteries? I need to know

What do you do with it?   Inside you   Where does it go?

---

* Williams, William Carlos, 1883-1963. *In the American Grain*. New York:
A. & C. Boni, 1925. p.74

Shipwreck Poem
by Anacaona Rocio Milagro

Do not look for a ship   in this poem   you will not find one—
just the wreck.

There is no mention of tumultuous sea journeys   or Tempests   or
Odysseus   or whales   or   the stomach of whales   —maybe remnants.

What torments the night   to make it dive and rip sails   will not be
unveiled —just the wreck.

Because this is a shipwreck poem   you will find   the ship
destroyed pieces repurposed—   bassinets made of driftwood, blood &
salvaged hope.
You will be enveloped by the stench of seaweed and vomit. You will find
a people   stuck.   Isolated.
In an environment not suited for long life. You will fall asleep hungry.
Awaken hungry. Spend the day with your stomach   burning   the rope
of your tongue.   You will be   chased.   You will   run   for your life   up
crumbling mountains   down filthy stairwells   live in crumbling housing
panic often   have night terrors in broad daylight.

Because so much of a shipwreck poem is to do with   delirium—a
common symptom of being   castaway.   You will find sanity in suicide.
Merciful. You will   keep the dead as friends.   Religion will be caught
between   fable, faith   and rage.   You will hear   screaming & crying.
Every so often you will find a floating body face down in the river   and
keep drinking.   You will build a raft of music   wax melded   broken
beats mended   needle & threaded into beautiful collages—
the world will listen in devotion but ignore the cry for help.

Let me tell you   how   little   is written   by   born castaways

Because this is   my   shipwreck poem   a 1980's baby   up the street of
New York City where i grew up   you'd find   a hollow library   where
my overdue mother   resorted   to fish-out books from the garbage   to
nourish   a young poet, an unwelcoming gated glowing-white Mansion

built on a high hill of indigenous skulls on unprotected looted
Lenape land, now sealed with landmark protection & immune to the
street avenues flooded by the war-on-drugs epidemic and the scattered
puddles of strung-out bodies and green glass bottles—emptiness the
note. You will find people substitute anything   for a boat.

For those of us born of this   wreckage   you will find   our muscles
sore —   spasms   from   unremembered storms. You will find   our
arms   like broken oars   make escape hard.   How we try   only to
redesign   the same disaster   because the   wreck   is
all we know.

Because this is   a shipwreck poem   most important of all   you will
find & face   an ocean   that swallows and hoards   all   that is meant
for you.

The Forgotten
by Naa Akua

Ask me what freedom is made of

Stirring the pot
a whisper   gun powder   Eliza Jumel's wishes
Summer homes to own buy and sell
Maybe make your slaves create a table to make sure
You are always at the head of it

My worries trapped in fickle payments knowing
that free never means sustainable
I sustain a rhythm so the food won't get clumped up before lunchtime
Hunched over with sweat every bead dropped is a prayer for my babies
For Solomon for time taken from this body that I may never get back

I am backed up by paperwork
But still feel enslaved
I am a surveillance of daydreams
shown through all dark brown eyes
And tattered skin

We don't belong in this story yet we are the reasons for its success
What an oxymoron even my ancestors chuckle
This notion of necessity and negligence
The blurring lines between   cattle   cargo   and teeth
and lips   and mouths   and arms   and legs
and feet   and stomachs   and hands

Wrangle them back to the pasture to work
Count them one   by   one
Until the sun sets
And we are all enveloped by the night
where there are no favorites
who circle around this mansion

Map of Northern Manhattan at the time of Colonization. The Morris-Jumel Mansion would later be constructed in the area near the "E" in Harlem. Credit: Illustrator Unknown, Townsend MacCoun (Publisher), "The Island of Manhattan (Mannahtin) at the Time of its Discovery," 1909, Courtesy of Lionel Pincus and Princess Firyal Map Division, The New York Public Library.

FRIENDS OF LAKE JACKSON

Florida

The mission of The Friends of Lake Jackson is to advocate for a common vision to preserve, enhance and maintain Lake Jackson and the Lake Jackson Basin ecosystems, habitats and natural functions.

We work to promote and support stewardship of Lake Jackson for recreation and use consistent with its ecological health. We also educate ourselves, residents, visitors and government agencies how to promote recreation that provides economic value while preserving, protecting and enhancing the lake's ecological health. And finally, The Friends of Lake Jackson coordinate private citizens, businesses and organizations, local, state and federal agencies to preserve and enhance the lake's ecological, recreational and economic value. www.FriendsofLakeJackson.org

-Poets:
- -Sandy Beck
- -Penelope Cornais
- -Jill Schrader
- -Tommy Dailey

-

Friends of Lake Jackson

The Friends of Lake Jackson was founded in 1998 by concerned citizens from all walks of life. We came together to be watchdogs for the lake and to act as a squeaky wheel at government meetings, and hearings on development, etc. The Board of Directors throughout the years has been comprised of retired biologists, geologists, hydrologists, botanists, master gardeners, hunters, lawyers, artists, photographers and more. We continue to advocate for the lake through education, outreach and collaboration. We strive to be a voice for the lake and most recently we have created a magazine called "The Lake Jackson Voice." Here are some excerpts from the inaugural March 2022 issue:

In March of 2019, just as many had witnessed for hundreds of years, Lake Jackson did disappear once again. After a long period of declining water levels, Lake Jackson entered a prolonged dry-down in early June 2021. During this period one of the two sinks in the lake, the Porter Hole Sink, emptied and refilled completely several times. Water remained in the upper and lower portions of the lake, and in isolated ponds around the sink, where fish and other aquatic creatures had a chance to survive if they managed to escape the huge flocks of birds that came to feed.

Photo (above): Porter Hole Sink in Dry Down with Water Level Marker Exposed by Terri Carrion

With the extensive dry down a new prairie habitat has emerged along with new flora and fauna that has thrived and adapted to the drier conditions. Also, the various government agencies that manage the lake have taken this opportunity to study the lake's geology in a new way. A dye trace was done through the sinkhole to show that the "disappearing waters" of Lake Jackson actually flow far and wide, down into the Floridan Aquifer and through the vast network of underground channels and caves, also passing through the renowned Wakulla Springs before finally making it out to the Gulf of Mexico. This data will help to secure Lake Jackson as an important water body to monitor more closely to ensure water quality is as clean and healthy as possible.

Lake Jackson continues to be an exciting place for birdwatching, as the periodic draining of Porter Hole Sink and its basin creates suitable habitat for shorebirds habitually not seen when the lake is at full pool. Unusual sightings, often reported on the eBird app of the Cornell Lab of Ornithology, have attracted a steady stream of expert birders, often at earlier and later hours, with the dry lakebed providing them at times with miles of walking and tracking.

Photo: Ibis Flocks in Winter by Terri Carrion

Two American Woodcocks were seen a number of times flying across and even landing about thirty minutes before sunrise at Miller Landing.

A couple of Short-eared Owls were seen and more recently, a Barn Owl was also reported for the first time in eleven years in Leon County at Faulk Dr. Landing and Miller Landing. These are in addition to the more common Barred Owls, Great Horned Owls, and rarer Eastern Screech-Owls, also reported.

Colorful warblers are currently being spotted, including a rare Blue-winged Warbler hybrid as well as a Blue-winged Warbler, and the more common Yellow Warblers, American Redstarts, Prairie Warblers, Black and White Warblers, Hooded Warblers, and others.

Photo: Juvenille Purple Gallinule and White Water Lily by Sandy Beck

Photo (above): Great Blue Heron by Sandy Beck
Photo (below): Snow Egret Moon Walking by Sandy Beck

Lake Jackson

Located five miles north of the center of Tallahassee, FL, Lake Jackson is a roughly 4,000 acre lake with a 27,000 acre watershed. Considered the "Jewel of Leon County," it has eight public landings and offers a myriad of recreational opportunities.

Lake Jackson was established as "Lake Jackson Aquatic Preserve" (LJAP) in 1973. Florida Aquatic Preserves are created to protect the aesthetic, ecological, cultural and scientific value of select water bodies. Lake Jackson is the only freshwater lake in Florida with that designation. It is also an "Outstanding Florida Water."

Defined as a perched lake, it is underlain by a thick layer of low permeability clay, which holds its water well above the regional groundwater limestone aquifer. As a closed basin, water enters as precipitation, runoff and differed surficial aquifer seepage. It exits through evaporation, and some leakage through the underlying clay strata and sinkholes. Water levels are always fluctuating making for a diverse and always shifting ecosystem.

Lake Jackson sits on the traditional territory of the Apalachee people. Evidence of the Fort Walton Culture of 1200 to 1500 is preserved at the Lake Jackson Archaeological Mounds State Park. They called the lake Okeeheepkee, meaning 'disappearing waters' due to the spontaneous draining of the lake through the two active sink holes.

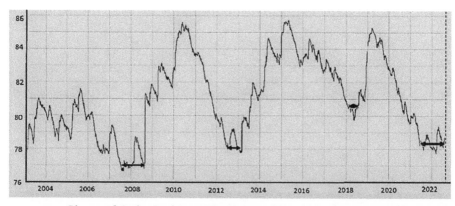

Chart of Lake Jackson Water Level by Alan Niedoroda

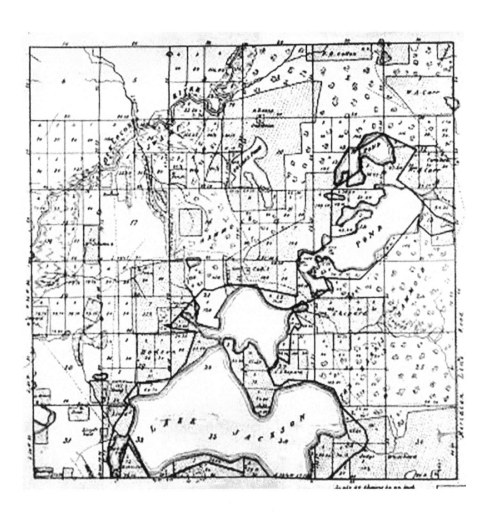

Excerpt of *Map of Lake Jackson area of Tallahassee, Florida, 1853.* 1853.
State Archives of Florida, Florida Memory.

They Called It Okeeheepkee
by Sandy Beck

Wrapped in morning mist, we slip into Lake Jackson.
Only Purple Gallinules, those brilliant rainbow birds,
prick sunrise stillness — cackling, laughing,
high stepping across water lilies.

An Osprey half flapping, half hovering fifty feet above our kayaks
plummets, smacking into the surface feet-first,
then rises on powerful strokes while spinning
its trophy bass headfirst. A very slick trick.

Snowy Egrets in bright yellow slippers slink along
the muddy shore, occasionally moon walking
to stir up breakfast, then perform a deep, croaky
song to impress close family and friends.

A softshell turtle pokes its long nose through duckweed.
Two Mississippi Kites pirouette overhead, plucking dragonflies
from the air that they swallow on the wing. We drift
past gangly, brown Limpkins — their haunting cries

competing with a distant Barred Owl — and one
adorable young gator that rests its head on a floating log,
four legs dangling in the current, until it slides
beneath my boat and drifts out of sight.

We've paddled this big lake for 34 years. Its wild lush
always dazzled me, until 10 billion gallons of water
slowly vaporized. And then one day — gone. It's natural,
I'm told, for this rain-fed lake dotted with sinkholes to vanish

every 20 years or so. Thirsty plants drink some and water oozes
through its sandy bottom. Add a drought, a dip in ground water
and a record heat wave then whoosh — Porter Sink seriously sucks.
So we hiked its muddy lake bed, past dead fish,

past decomposing aquatic plants, past a frenzy of feasting gulls
to the disappearing water spectacle: billions of gallons gushing
into the Florida Aquifer. Imagine the Colorado River raging
with spring snowmelt and its explosive sound. That's it.

A Spanish priest who visited our lake in 1716 described
a prairie where hundreds of buffalo grazed. Yes, buffalo.
The Natives he met called it Okeeheepkee — "disappearing waters."

Signs of climate change in Alaska are dramatic. Glaciers melt
and retreat daily. In Florida, we have deadly heat waves, catastrophic
hurricanes and this lake — that used to disappear every 20 years. But
that's history. It's already Okeeheepkeed three times this year.

Where we once launched our kayaks, a rare Short-eared Owl showed up
to hunt rats and marsh rabbits. Thrilled to our toes, we watched it float
moth-like above the tall grass and dry lake bed. No wild lush
to paddle now. Just a dazzling prairie of wildflowers and a sea of change.

Photo: Adult Purple Gallinule by Sandy Beck

The Lake with No Water
by Penelope Cornais

The lake with a sink hole
Lake Jackson
A lake with no water
So many interesting birds
Frog eggs scattered in piles
for some predator to eat
The scooped-out bowls in the mud where fish once laid eggs
Dead fish left to rot in other places
Small waterfalls that we leapt over as if we were hobbits
We return to school with our shoes, socks and pants covered in mud

Photo: Dry Lake Bed by Sandy Beck

Photo: Bluegill Nests Exposed During Dry Down by Terri Carrion

Photo (above): Young Gater Hanging On Log by Sandy Beck
Photo (below): Lake Jackson by Terri Carrion

If I Was a Tree
by Jill Schrader

If I was a tree
I'd feel each bright green leaf
Marvel at my curving branches
Send each root deep into the earth
If I was a tree
I'd be home to many
Frogs and lizards nestled in my roots
Birds and owls would make their homes
In my leafy canopy
If I was a tree
I'd feel the wind part my branches
Let the water rush up my roots
And into my trunk
If I was a tree

Photo: Limpkin at Lake Jackson by Sandy Beck

Photo (above): Lake Jackson by Terri Carrion
Photo (below): Porter Hole Sink Drains to Expose Cavernous
Lake Bottom by Terri Carrion

A Beautiful Memory
by Tommy Dailey

Fields of grass,
where a lake once was.
The wind whistled and swayed,
yet no clouds in the sky.
A small stream flows over limestone,
seeing sunlight first time in decades.
Mud up to our knees,
Fresh air down in our lungs.
Yes, the lake was gone,
but it would be back;
we were sure.

Photo: Lake Jackson Wildflower Prairie by Sandy Beck

Photo (above): Finch, Ellis. *Two boys fishing on Lake Jackson in Leon County.* 1965. State Archives of Florida, Florida Memory.
Photo (below): Bob Beck Paddling by Sandy Beck

Poets' Biographies

Naa Akua is a New York born poet, actor, educator, and sound-word practitioner who is Ghanaian/Bajan and queer. Akua uses the vibratory energy of sound and the intent of word as a vehicle towards healing. Akua, former 2019 Citizen University Poet-in-Residence is a Liberal Arts Teacher at Achievement First East Brooklyn High School, Hugo House teacher, and Young Women Empowered (Y-WE) youth facilitator.

Sandy Beck is a writer, teacher and wildlife advocate. As St. Francis Wildlife's education director, she cares for the disabled hawks and owls that accompany her to events and schools. She published *Conserving Florida Wildlife,* a Middle School Curriculum and several collections of poetry about native birds by local students. As a Women's History Month honoree, Sandy was named one of the ten 'Women Taking the Lead to Save Our Planet.'

Ben Bentele
Fruit Fly. Folksinger. Storyteller. Hay-Hand. Translator.
Ex-physicist. Orchard tech. bbben.org

For over 30 years, **Michael Brandt** has contributed poems and commentary across a spectrum of midwestern news and special interest publications. In 2020, his work was included in the anthology *Contours, A Literary Landscape,* published by the Driftless Writing Center. He shares a home overlooking the Wisconsin River valley with his wife Janet and their large hound.

Penelope Cornais is a 7th grade student at Raa Middle School and loves science, reading and writing. She won a writing award from the Big Bend Area Literacy Council and was published in their anthology in 2016. Her writing has also been featured on the *Fabled Kids* Podcast in 2020. She is a currently a middle school research fellow for the National High Magnetic Field Laboratory. Instagram: @nelas_journal

Tommy Dailey is an 8th grader at Raa Middle School where he participates on the football team and the advanced steel drum band. He was elected president of the STEAM Club, and is a member of the Shop Club, Scouts, and the Faith Presbyterian Church Youth Group. He enjoys animé, Dungeons & Dragons, and water sports.

CMarie Fuhrman is a poet, nonfiction writer, educator, and future ancestor. CMarie is Associate Director of the Graduate Program in Creative Writing at Western Colorado University and directs the Elk River Writers Workshop. She lives with dogs and a fish biologist in West Central Idaho where she hikes, camps, and serves as Idaho's Writer in Resident. CMarieFuhrman.com

Margaret Gibson, State Poet Laureate of Connecticut (2019-2022), is the author of 13 books of poems from LSU Press, including most recently *Not Hearing the Wood Thrush,* 2018, and *The Glass Globe*, 2021. Awards include the Lamont Selection for Long Walks in the Afternoon; the Melville Kane Award, the Connecticut Book Award, and a Pushcart Prize. Gibson is Professor Emerita, University of Connecticut. margaretgibsonpoetry.com

Vicki Graham is the author of 3 collections of poetry, *Alembic* (finalist for the Minnesota Book Award), *The Tenderness of Bees*, and *The Hummingbird's Tongue.* She has been writer in residence at the H. J. Andrews Experimental Forest and writer/witness of clear cutting at Shotpouch Creek. Retired professor of English and environmental studies at the University of Minnesota, she now lives in Oregon and is a regular contributor of poetry to the Audubon newsletter, *Storm Petrel.*

Anacaona Rocio Milagro is a poet born, raised and living in NYC. She earned an MFA in Poetry at NYU Paris, an MPH at Columbia University and a BA in Anthropology/Journalism at Baruch College. A Cave Canem Fellow, a Nuyorican Poets Café National Teammate, she's published in *Narrative Magazine, The BreakBeat Poets Anthology, The Common,* and others. Her track "Stillmatic" is on streaming platforms. Her mother is from St.Thomas and father from Dominican Republic. IG @poet.anacaona

Cathleen Miller is an artist, writer, herbalist and small-scale herb farmer living on Wabanaki land near the Nonesuch River in Scarborough, Maine. She is happiest when she has her hands in the dirt and has time to listen to the birds chatter in the trees. Cathleen is passionate about the power of connection to the land and all of our non-human neighbors to heal our spirits and bodies. She spends her days working as an archivist and sometimes publishes poems and essays in journals and anthologies.

Stacy Boe Miller is a poet and essay writer living in northern Idaho. Some of her work can be found in *River Teeth Beautiful Things, Mid-American Review, Terrain.org, Copper Nickel,* and other journals. She serves on the board of *High Desert Journal* and is currently the Poet Laureate of the city of Moscow.

Claire Millikin is the author of nine books of poetry, including *After Houses-Poetry for the Homeless* (2014), *Television* (2016), *State Fair Animals* (2018) and *Dolls* (2021). Millikin is a 2021 recipient of the Maine Literary Award. Millikin's book *Dolls* is a 2022 semifinalist for the PSV Poetry Book Award for North American Publishers & Writers. As Claire Raymond, she publishes scholarship, emphasizing feminist visual culture, and teaches for the University of Maine.

Michaeline Picaro is a member of the Ramapough Lunaape Nation Turtle Clan, and a traditionalist with knowledge of medicinal plants. She is a co-founder of the Munsee Three Sisters Medicinal Farm, and a co-founder of Ramapough Culture and Land Foundation. Michaeline also carries the Clan Mother title. She is a Tribal Historic Preservation Officer for the Ramapough Lenape Nation, Turtle Clan and preservationist for ceremonial landscapes.

Danny Rosen founded Lithic Press and has run Lithic Bookstore & Gallery in Fruita, CO since it opened in 2015. Early on he learned to swing a hammer which has been most helpful throughout his career in carpentry, geology, astronomy, education and especially as a publisher. Most mornings he pisses into the largest unnamed tributary to the East Branch of Big Salt Wash which flushes into the Colorado River. His latest book is *The Tuscan Journals & Other Poems* (Cuneiform Press, 2022.)

Holly Russell's poems and essays have been published at *The Ogham Stone 2022, Hibiscus: poems that heal and empower, Literary Mama, The Good Men Project, Pendemic, Gaining Ground, Darien Pollinator Pathway, Poets Respond Live, The Irish Echo, NJ.com, StamfordAdvocate, Motherwell Magazine, All Things Alison,* and *Smyth County VA Tourism*. She teaches at Building One Community in Stamford, CT, and founded Holly's Greetings LLC, featuring her poems and photographs. holly-russell.com @holleeerussell

Erin Schneider, M.ED co-owns and stewards Hilltop Community Farm in La Valle, WI specializing in organic fruit and flowers. She has written for and been featured in various local, regional, and international publications, as a Farmer/Writer in Residence at Michigan State University's Kellogg Biological Research Center, as a Community Artist for Fermentation Festival Farm/Art Dtour, World Farmer Organization's *F@rmletters, National Geographic,* and agricultural trade journals.

Jill Schrader is a seventh grader at Augusta Raa Middle School. Her hobbies include writing, acting, coding, and art. She is writing a sci-fi / fantasy book and hopes to have it published. Jill was first published in Gilchrist Elementary School's literary magazine.

Alexandra Teague is the author of the poetry collections *Or What We'll Call Desire, The Wise and Foolish Builders,* and *Mortal Geography,* and the novel *The Principles Behind Flotation*. She is also co-editor of the anthologies *Bullets into Bells: Poets & Citizens Respond to Gun Violence* and *Broadsided Press: Fifteen Years of Poetic and Artistic Collaboration*. The recipient of awards including The California Book Award and an NEA Fellowship, she is a professor at University of Idaho.

Rosemerry Wahtola Trommer co-hosts *Emerging Form*, a podcast on creative process, and is co-founder of *Secret Agents of Change*, a surreptitious kindness cabal. Her poetry has appeared in *O Magazine,* on *A Prairie Home Companion* and *PBS News Hour,* in *Rattle.com* and in Ted Kooser's *American Life in Poetry*. She has 13 books of poetry. *Hush* won the Halcyon Prize for poems of human ecology. wordwoman.com

Tammi J Truax has worked as a teacher in a variety of settings, co-founded The Prickly Pear Poetry Project, was editor of *The Poet's Tale; Lady Wentworth* (2013), and author of *Broken Buckets* (2013) and a YA novel in verse *For to See the Elephant* (2019). Her poetry has appeared in 14 anthologies, and in journals, newspapers, and online. She was the Maine Beat Poet Laureate for two years and the Portsmouth (NH) Poet Laureate for three years, with a project featured in *The New York Times*.

Lisa "Rubi G." Ventura (she/her) is a Washington Heights-bred Black Dominican poet and essayist, a first-generation daughter of immigrants, a mother, and has been published by *Dominican Writers, Raising Mothers*, and *Economic Hardship Program in conjunction with Slate*, among others. She was interviewed for The Nation's *Going for Broke* podcast series and Refinery29's *Somos*. Lisa has served as an empowerment panelist and is a VONA alumni. www.lapoetarubi.com or @poeta_rubi_g.

Wendy Videlock is recipient of 4 Keats Soul-Making Prizes. Her poems, reviews, and essays appear widely, most notably in *Poetry, O Magazine, Hudson Review, Best American Poetry, Hopkins Review, The New York Times*, and *American Life in Poetry*. Her most recent books are a collection of essays, *The Poetic Imaginarium: A Worthy Difficulty* (Lithic Press), and a new collection of poems, *Wise to the West* (Able Muse Press). wendy-videlock.constantcontactsites.com

Artists' Biographies

Martin Bridge (cover artist) carries his family tradition forth as he lives, creates and teaches in Western Massachusetts. His work spans a wide range of media: Drawing, Painting, Sculpture, Theater Design, Site Specific Installations, and Performance. As an avid Permaculture designer he strives to improve his awareness of how he relates to the natural world and to live in better balance. Through his work he hopes to inspire and cultivate a greater sense of mystery and possibility. thebridgebrothers.com

Terri Carrion is Board President of the Friends of Lake Jackson. She is a writer, artist, and yoga instructor who loves to photograph nature and is lucky enough to have Lake Jackson as her backyard. As co-founder of *100 Thousand Poets for Change*, she is always eager to collaborate and to connect the arts and nature to help bring more attention to the importance of environmental sustainability. She is also Board President of Anhinga Press.

Marty Espinola is a retired educator who is also a widely published photographer. He wants to make use of the images he captures to benefit groups and individuals who care for the planet and each other. He still hopes we all have a chance if we work together. He can be contacted at martyesp1@yahoo.com

Jack Jensen is President of Jensen Machine Company in Newington, CT, and is also an amateur photographer. He began flying ultra-light aircraft in 2007 and has spent many happy hours flying over the Great Meadows, Connecticut River, and the surrounding area.

Dan Kehlenbach is a passionate nature photographer who can be found wandering through wetlands, forests, and shorelines exploring the wonder and beauty of the natural world.

Tim Lewis is past president of Great Meadows Conservation Trust, Inc. and is currently a trustee of the Connecticut River Conservancy. Tim believes the Great Meadows and the Connecticut River go hand in hand. The river created and maintains the meadows with its flows and spring freshets, and the meadows attract birds and other wildlife along the river's shore. Tim leads paddles on the river for Connecticut Trails Day, and is often found on the water.

Phil Lohman's career spanned decades as graphic artist for the *Hartford Courant*, drawing his trademark sketch maps of Hartford's neighborhoods. His maps of historic Old Wethersfield and the meadows adorn Heritage Walk signs guiding tourists and residents through the village and through the changes over time in the village, and the meanderings of the Connecticut River through the Great Meadows.

Abby Wilson enjoys hiking, photographing wildlife, snowshoeing, and swimming. She has worked as a whale watch naturalist in the Gulf of Maine, a snowshoe guide in the mountains of Western Maine, a zipline instructor in the Southern Berkshires of Massachusetts, an assistant land steward on Mount Desert Island, a digital media intern with the Northeast Wilderness Trust in Vermont, and as an Education Specialist with the Scarborough Land Trust.

Jim Woodworth is a past president and Stewardship Chair of the The Great Meadows Conservation Trust, Inc.. He also edits the newsletter *The Meadow View*, where he illustrates stories with his photographs of trust activities, including work sessions, Winter Walks which he often leads, and scenes from the meadows.

About Lis McLoughlin (editor)

Lis McLoughlin holds a BS in Civil Engineering, an MEd in Education, and a PhD in Science and Technology Studies. She founded NatureCulture LLC (nature-culture.net) a green, online media and events company through which she directs the Writing the Land project (writingtheland.org), and edits and publishes the Writing the Land anthologies, as well as other books. Her own published works include edited anthologies; academic articles; poems; essays; a stage performance; book chapters; and newspaper articles. Lis organizes the annual Authors and Artists Festival, and serves on the Northfield (Massachusetts) Historical Commission. She lives off-grid in Northfield, Massachusetts and part-time in Montréal, Québec.

About Susan Cerulean (foreword)

For more than three decades, Susan Cerulean has kayaked, hiked, scalloped, fished and counted birds on and around Dog, the St. Georges and St Vincent islands. She is author of *I Have Been Assigned the Single Bird: A Daughter's Memoir* (2020); *Coming to Pass: Florida's Coastal Islands in a Gulf of Change* (2015) which was awarded a Gold Medal for Florida Nonfiction by the Florida Book Awards; and *Tracking Desire: A Journey after Swallow-tailed Kites* (2005), which was named Editor's Choice by Audubon magazine. Cerulean has traveled from Standing Rock Reservation to St. Vincent Island, encouraging people to understand the linkages between our human choices and the state of the Earth, particularly climate change. She designed the state of Florida's Nongame and Watchable Wildlife Programs before turning to a full-time writing and speaking. Her essays, editorials and poems have appeared widely.

Lightning Source UK Ltd.
Milton Keynes UK
UKHW012007010223
416340UK00005B/25